9 TO 5 BEATS TEN TO LIFE

How to (Re) Enter Society, 2ⁿᵈ Edition

Revised and Updated

Mike S. Davis, M.A.

FOUNDED 1870

Mission of the American Correctional Association

The American Correctional Association provides a professional organization for all individuals and groups, both public and private, that share a common goal of improving the justice system.

American Correctional Association Staff

Harold C. Clarke, President
James A. Gondles, Jr., CAE, Executive Director
Gabriella M. Klatt, Director, Communications and Publications
Alice Heiserman, Manager of Publications and Research
Jeannelle Ferreira, Associate Editor
Xavaire Bolton, Graphics and Production Associate
Cover design by Xavaire Bolton
Printed in the United States of America by Gasch Printing, LLC

Artwork and Photograph Credits

Michael Ryan, Artist
O'Lamar Gibson, Artist
Ben Aveling, Artist
Missouri Department of Corrections
Piaggio Group USA for Vespa
U.S. Fish and Wildlife Service
U.S. Office of War Information
Wikimedia Commons
Mike S. Davis
Elvert Xavier Barnes Photography

U.S. Navy Seaman Kelly E. Barnes
Thomas Berg
Michael Deschenes
Gunnery Sergeant R. L. Jaggard
Sekhar Lukose Kuriakose
Christophe Meneboeuf
Dennis Mojado
Lauren Valdes

ISBN: 978-1-56991-311-6

The Inside Stuff

You do not need to read this manual cover-to-cover. Use bits and pieces that apply to your situation.

Been There Done That

When the editor of this book asked if I were interested in updating and revising it, my immediate response was "No." I said, "I've been there, done that; besides, every time I put a copy of the first edition in the probation and parole office where I work, it is stolen." The editor replied, "Well, then, maybe offenders still need and want this information." As a result, here is the updated version. It has many new sources of information and is based on the experience of many ex-offenders.

Special thanks to...

Panera™ Bread at Red Mill, in Virginia Beach, for not booting me out, allowing me to spend numerous hours at their café/bakery, while sipping an all-day Coke and writing the revisions to this book.

If You Only Read One Page of This Book, Read This

If you live in North America, you are fortunate. If you commit a crime in North America, you are fortunate. Why? The criminal justice system is far more lenient than in third-world countries. My travels have taken me overseas, where I have witnessed, first hand, terrible, inhumane incarceration conditions. Many of these seem straight from your worst nightmares. Imagine being in a 16 x 16-foot cell with fifty-seven other women who are hot, thirsty, hungry, and tired, where tempers flare and people get hurt. How about being a young man, incarcerated for four years in stifling, dirty conditions, still waiting for his sentence? You will not find educational programs, pre-release classes, or halfway houses in these countries. If you are a felon, you may as well be a leper, or you might just disappear. You will not find job opportunities for ex-felons in many other criminal justice systems.

Yes, we live in a country that offers second chances, where, if you have committed a felony, you will face obstacles. However, with diligence and perseverance, you have the ability to overcome your circumstances.

I should have prepared!

Introduction

As much as things have changed since the initial publication of this book, just as much has remained the same. The country is in the midst of great economic turmoil. The cost of gas has escalated to almost $4.00 a gallon, the war in Iraq is past its eighth year, 2.2 million homes are in foreclosure. If that is not bad enough, McDonald's raised the price of its ice cream cones by 10 cents. On a positive note, the first African-American President of the United States was elected.

What has remained the same is what ex-offenders need upon their release from incarceration: jobs, housing, and supportive services. Correctional institutions that recognize these needs are offering more pre-release classes for ex-offenders approaching their release date, to better prepare them for their release and successful reintegration. In addition, the Second Chance Act is now law. This legislation provides funding to government entities, community-based organizations, and faith-based groups so that they can expand or develop reentry services.

Perhaps the greatest change in the past ten years is the emergence of computers and the Internet. The Internet makes information readily available, and provides another, easier means of securing employment, housing, and every type of support service you need. Increasingly, companies are listing job openings on the Internet. This allows the job seeker to conduct searches and complete job applications with greater ease than traditional job-search methods. As a result, many employers no longer accept walk-ins to inquire about jobs or to fill out applications. Increasingly, employers will contact you through e-mail and make an appointment for an interview if you meet their requirements. We are aware that most inmates do not have access to a computer and if they do, certainly not the Internet. However, you can apply this information when you return to the community.

Many excellent books on job finding are written by ex-offenders. While this author is not an ex-offender, he has worked in halfway houses, community organizations, and currently as a probation and parole officer, helping ex-offenders transition from prison to the community. This book is a bit "edgy and snappy." The author believes that ex-offenders, as a rule, are not suited to traditional jobs in mainstream society. They tend to prefer jobs that are non-traditional, somewhat dangerous, adventurous, and exciting. Many of these jobs are listed in the book. This book goes way beyond just getting a job, and includes sections on self-employment and becoming an entrepreneur. You will be encouraged to find your passion and pursue your life's work. Whether a reader is incarcerated or on probation, the same principles apply and you can use them. This is an interactive book. You cannot just sit back and read it, but should take an active role and participate.

This book is meant to inspire and motivate you. Ex-offenders face many barriers, but armed with the right information and perseverance, opportunities do exist.

Mike Davis

FOR THE FACILITATOR

This *9 to 5 Beats Ten to Life* workbook is a step-by-step, interactive approach to fundamental skills needed for the ex-offender to obtain and maintain a job. Use this book to actively engage ex-cons in their own employment and educational process. Studies indicate that if ex-offenders are gainfully employed, their chances of recidivism are greatly decreased.

This approach goes beyond merely obtaining a job. It explores available educational opportunities for skill development to help ex-offenders move beyond basic employment. Besides traditional employment, this book provides information about dangerous, adventurous, and non-traditional jobs that may appeal to the offender population. We put strong emphasis on career exploration and how to choose a vocation that matches their interests and skills. In addition, this book presents information and resources regarding housing, transportation, and community services.

This book begins with a work-assessment quiz to determine the current knowledge base of ex-offenders, probationers, or parolees. After they complete the assessment, instructors can use successive pages for their daily lesson plans to teach new skill sets. Each lesson consists of one-to-two pages. Instructors also should familiarize themselves with resources in their own communities and offer suggestions to supplement those discovered by offenders. By reading material aloud and discussing it in a group format, you may use this manual with a variety of educational levels.

This book is not intended only for instructors in a prison classroom setting. Many ex-offenders who have been released from correctional facilities may not have had the opportunity to participate in pre-release classes. Community social service agencies that provide employment classes to the offender population also can use this book. The self-motivated ex-offender may benefit by using this book as an avenue of self-directed learning. The video/DVD of *9 to 5 Beats Ten to Life* (available from the Amercian Correctional Association) may be used in conjunction with this book as a visual aid.

What makes this book unique is matching a person's talents and passions with a career. The author provides details about entrepreneurial options and adventurous jobs. Ex-offenders are urged to consider their training and education to help them reach their goals. While female offenders may use all of the information, their unique concerns are addressed in a separate chapter.

To help the offenders sustain themselves on the outside, some practical advice is presented on job interviews, first jobs, temporary jobs, and leaving a job. Then, the author provides information on community resources, including options for housing and sources for books in prison. An annotated bibliography offers some suggestions and inspirational sources for further exploration—again something that offenders can begin while incarcerated.

At the conclusion of the book, you may use the initial test (on page xii) as a post-release quiz to gauge whether the ex-offender, parolee, or probationer has grasped the necessary skills to successfully obtain and maintain a job. In other words, is this material working? We would be interested in having researchers at universities also evaluate this material to prove that it makes a difference in the recidivism rate of those who use this material compared with those who do not.

PRE-EMPLOYMENT ASSESSMENT: WHAT DO YOU KNOW?

This quiz is meant to gauge your knowledge about employment. At the end of the book, you will have a follow-up quiz to see what you have learned.

1. What two forms of identification do you need to work legally in the United States?
   _____
   _____

2. What is an employment portfolio and what is its purpose?
   _____
   _____
   _____

3. What are three ways to find job leads?
   _____
   _____
   _____

4. What is the Federal Bonding Program?
   _____

5. How do you get a certified copy of your birth certificate?
   _____

6. What are three expectations employers may have?
   _____
   _____
   _____

7. What is a Targeted Tax Credit for employers?
   _____

8. What four things can you do prior to your release to prepare for a job?
   _____   _____
   _____   _____

9. What is an apprenticeship program?
   _____

10. With a criminal record, are you prohibited from working for yourself?
    _____

11. What is the Oxford House?
    _____

12. What is the quickest way to find a job?

_____

_____

_____

_____

13. Large companies, such as Target or Home Depot, are the best places to apply for jobs?

    True or False

14. Name three organizations that could assist you in your reintegration.

_____

_____

_____

15. What is the minimum recommended time to stay on the job before moving on to another one?

_____

16. How are you going to answer the question, "Have you ever been convicted of a crime?"

_____

_____

_____

17. What industries are more apt to hire felons?

_____   _____

_____   _____

18. What are three ways to improve your knowledge and skills?

_____

_____

_____

19. What is a one-stop career center?

_____

20. What is a search engine?

_____

I should have planned!

DO YOU HAVE A PLAN?

IT IS NEVER TOO SOON TO PREPARE

This scenario happens over and over again. An ex-offender came to see me, his probation officer. He had left the correctional facility that morning with only "gate money."

**He had NO identification,
NO employment prospects,
and NO housing.**

It does NOT have to be that way!

Start preparing for employment now!

This scenario happens over and over. A newly released ex-offender comes into the office in a panic. "I need an ID. I can't get a job without one." That's right. You can't!

Since the tragedy of September 11, 2001, obtaining state identification is difficult. Companies are required by law to complete an I-9 form for all new hires to prove that they are eligible to work in the United States.

Many others before you have become employed, and so can you!

YOUR PLAN?

A football team does not show up on a Sunday afternoon ready to play. They prepare and plan for that game during the week. A boxer trains for hundreds of hours prior to a bout. Even the writing of this book, *9 to 5 Beats Ten to Life*, took thought, research, and organization before the author put one word on paper.

Go ahead and answer each of the following questions. Which ones offer challenges you have not considered?

- How prepared are you for your release?

- Do you have a certified copy of your birth certificate?
  If not, how do you get one?

- Where are you going to live?

- What means of transportation will you have?

- At what companies will you apply for a job?

- How are you going to explain your criminal record?

- Would you rather wait until you hit the streets to make a plan
  or be ready now, before your release?

We will answer many of these questions and others in this book.
Do what you can **now**!

A SUCCESS STORY

Alex was incarcerated for four years. He was released at 9:30 A.M., and hired the same afternoon as a cook. Alex accepted the position, but now he had a dilemma: what to do with the eight other job interviews he had scheduled.

How did he do it? First of all, he applied himself while he was incarcerated. He participated in all the educational and counseling classes offered by his correctional institution, and he planned for his future.

Secondly, Alex put together a resume, found job leads in the classified ads, and sent out his resume, along with a cover letter. He was interested in working in food service, so he wrote to numerous restaurants in the area in which he would be living. Not all responded, but Alex maintained contact with those that did, gave them his release date, and stated that he would like to stop at the restaurant for an interview upon his release.

Do You Have a Plan?

Alex's actual job cover letter and resume, as he sent them to employers, follows.

Alex Goforth
7525 4th Avenue
Lino Lakes, MN 55014
(612) 555-6667
alexgoforth@gmail.net

February 5

Bon Appetit Restaurant
12 S 6th St, Suite 616
Minneapolis, MN 55402

Dear Sir or Madam:

I am responding to your recent ad in the *Star Tribune*. I believe that I am well qualified for the position of cook, and I know I could make a significant contribution to your company.

Although I have enclosed my resume, let me quickly highlight some of my relevant experiences. Through my in-depth cooking jobs at various places, I have had hands-on experience working in restaurants and food service. I have had experience in the areas of management, inventory control, and communication.

I hope that we will be able to meet in person to discuss the cook position. If I don't hear from you next week, I will give you a call during the week of February 17 to inquire if I might make an appointment. I look forward to speaking with you soon.

I will be available for interviews after February 10. You can either write to me or leave a message at the following phone number: (612) 555-6667.

Sincerely,

Alex Goforth

Alex Goforth

Enc: Resume

7525 4th Ave.,
Lino Lakes, MN 5014
(612) 555-6667
alexgoforth@gmail.net

Alex Goforth

Objective	Cook position. To secure full-time cook position with the desire for advancement to a chef's position.
Experience	Over the past 20 years, I have had various experience working in restaurants and food services from prep to fry and line cooking, to catering cafeteria style. Also, I have managed and maintained an extension library, which gave me experience in management, inventory control, and communication.
Education	General Education Development Certificate Minnesota Literary Council (MLC) Tutor Certificate Over 1,500 hours as MLC Tutor Experience with both PC and Macintosh computers Successfully completed Critical Thinking Course Rassmussen Business College Metropolitan State University (31 college credits) Minneapolis Technical College Course Overview Introduction to Food Service Table Service 1 and 2 Introduction to Pantry Food Preparation Basic Cooking Principles Introduction to Breakfast Foods Basic Baking Basic Food Production Principles Quality Assurance Institutional Food Production Restaurant Hotel Food Production
References	Available upon request

HOW TO PREPARE FOR A JOB ON THE OUTSIDE WHILE INSIDE

THINGS YOU NEED TO GET A JOB

	HAVE	NEED
✓ State ID	❏	❏
✓ Birth Certificate		
✓ Social Security Card	❏	❏
✓ Master Application	❏	❏
✓ Job Evaluations	❏	❏
✓ GED, Diploma	❏	❏
✓ Transcript of Grades	❏	❏
✓ Photographs of Your Work	❏	❏
✓ Vocational School Certificate	❏	❏
✓ Treatment Certificates	❏	❏
✓ Appointment with an Employment Counselor	❏	❏
✓ Information on Federal Bonding	❏	❏
✓ Information on Targeted Tax Credits	❏	❏
✓ Housing	❏	❏
✓ Clothing for Your Interview	❏	❏
✓ Phone Number or Answering Service	❏	❏
✓ E-Mail Address	❏	❏

NO ID, NO JOB

1. START WITH A BIRTH CERTIFICATE

To obtain a state identification card, you will need to obtain a certified copy of your birth certificate. To get your certified birth certificate, write to the Vital Statistics Office in the state in which you were born. Include the following:

✓ Full name, as it appears on the birth certificate

✓ City and state where you were born

✓ Date of birth

✓ Gender

✓ Mother's maiden name

✓ Father's full name

Fees for this document vary from $10.00 to $20.00 (subject to change). The appendix of this book lists state contacts for vital documents.

2. GET A STATE ID OR DRIVER'S LICENSE

To get your state ID or a driver's license, contact your state's department of motor vehicles or driver's license department. If you have Internet access, www.dmv.org lists each state's office and requirements. Often, two or more other forms of identification are required, and may include a state or federal correctional identification card.

3. OBTAIN A SOCIAL SECURITY CARD

If you do not have a Social Security card, or do not remember the number, write to your regional office of the Department of Health and Human Services, listed in the *Yellow Pages* under Federal Government. Or, write to the Social Security Administration's national office:

Social Security Administration
Office of Disclosure
Policy 3-A-6
Operations Building
6401 Security Blvd.
Baltimore, MD 21235

1 (800) 772-1313   www.ssa.gov

They will send you an application form and a return envelope. There is no charge to apply for a Social Security card.

You may also want to request a print-out of your job history. This will be valuable when you complete your master application.

This process can take up to twelve weeks. So, get started EARLY!

4. RETRIEVE YOUR MILITARY DISCHARGE PAPERS

Veterans and their families may obtain a copy of the service member's DD-214, Certificate of Release or Discharge from Active Duty, from the National Archives:

The National Archives and Records Administration
8601 Adelphi Rd.
College Park, MD 20740-6001
1(866) 272-6272 or 1-86-NARA-NARA
Fax (301) 837-0483

Whether you request your records using a Standard Form SF-180 or a letter, you must **sign, date,** and mail the document to the following address:

National Personnel Records Center
Military Personnel Records
9700 Page Ave.
St. Louis, MO 63132-5100

Your SF-180 or letter of request must contain certain basic information, including:
- Your complete name used while in service
- Service number
- Social Security number
- Branch of service
- Dates of service
- Date and place of birth (especially if the service number is not known).
- If you suspect your records may have been involved in the 1973 fire, also include:
  - o Place of discharge
  - o Last unit of assignment
  - o Place of entry into the service, if known.
- All requests must be signed and dated by the veteran or next-of-kin.

The National Personnel Records Center normally responds to requests for separation documents (such as DD Form 214) in ten working days or less. However, requests that involve reconstruction efforts due to the 1973 fire may take much longer. You will receive a response in writing by U.S. Mail.

(Source: www.archives.gov)

5. If necessary, get an ALIEN REGISTRATION CARD

If you are not a U.S. citizen and have misplaced your Permanent Resident I-551 (green card) or other documentation proving your right to work in the United States, contact your local Immigration and Naturalization Services office, listed in the telephone book as Citizenship and Immigration Services or Immigration and Customs Enforcement, and they will help you apply for a replacement card by filing a USCIS Form I-90. If you do not have access to e-filing (Internet) for these forms, mail them to a regional service center. Your local office can direct you to the right one.

Start getting ready to find a job while in prison. This way, when you are released, you immediately have everything employers require.

CREATE A PORTFOLIO!

A portfolio is a collection of documents, such as class completion certificates, diplomas, letters of recommendation, and other items that show you in a good light. It shows your achievements and demonstrates your motivation while incarcerated. The goal: show a potential employer what you have accomplished during your incarceration. It will help you during your job search.

WHAT IS IN A PORTFOLIO?

PERSONAL

- Certified birth certificate
- Social Security card
- DD214—Military Discharge

EDUCATIONAL

- GED certificate or high school diploma
- Vocational training certificates
- Post-secondary diplomas/certificates
- Transcript of grades
- Certificates of completion from chemical-dependency, parenting, job-seeking, counseling, or other classes

WORK

- Mistake-free application
- Job evaluations
- Resume
- Letters of recommendation
- Photographs of your work
- Awards/certificates

AFTER RELEASE, ADD INFORMATION ABOUT

- Federal bonding
- Targeted tax credit

Certificate of Completion

This certifies that

_____

has successfully completed the (14 week)
Phase I & Phase II
Substance Abuse
Psycho-Educational Program
offered at Greensville Correctional Center

Jerome Spearman SIRC   4-14-00
Signature   Program Facilitator   Date

_____
Signature   Program Facilitator   Date

Commonwealth of Virginia

THIS IS TO CERTIFY THAT

_____
NAME

Having mastered the necessary skills
is qualified to seek employment in the following **3**
Job title(s) as defined in the Dictionary of Occupational Titles.

763-381-010   Furniture Finisher   763-684-038   Furniture Assembler

769-687-054   Wood working Shop Hand

_____   _____
Instructor   Superintendent of Schools   Principal

9-3-02
Date

This is a Certificate of Course Completion – Not a License

Valid Only When Embossed With "OFFICIAL COPY" Seal

HOW DO YOU LOOK ON PAPER?

- **APPLICATIONS**
- **RESUMES**

COMPLETING APPLICATIONS

"Filling out an application is like taking a test."

■ Ex-offender

"Before I interview an applicant, I like to see a completed application, including references."

■ Employer

A typical application includes:

- Former employers' company names

- Supervisors' names, telephone numbers, and e-mail addresses

- Address with ZIP code [ZIP code information is available at http://zip4.usps.com or by calling (800) 275-8777]

- Titles of jobs you held

- Companies' telephone numbers

- Current descriptions of jobs you have held

Prepare a mistake-free application on pages 18-19.

Take this application with you during your job hunt, and copy this information onto the employer's application.

It takes *time and effort* to complete a mistake-free application, but preparation now will help you on your job search later!

Application 1

1. Are you working now .... ☒No ☐Yes - Hours per week: _____   Hourly Wage: _____
2. If married, is your spouse employed .. ☒No ☐Yes - Hours per week: _____   Hourly Wage: _____
3. If unemployed, did you receive a termination/layoff notice .... ☒No ☐Yes - Date received: _____
4. Unemployment compensation status .... ☐Eligible Claimant ☐Not Eligible ☐Claim Exhausted
5. Are you able to work: ☒Yes ☐No - If not, why _____
6. What have you been doing since your last job _Incarceration_ 84-89 89-91

LIST YOUR WORK EXPERIENCE COMPLETELY STARTING WITH YOUR PRESENT OR MOST RECENT JOB

COMPANY NAME: Preffered temp ①   **ADDRESS:**   **SUPERVISOR:**

JOB TITLE:

YOUR JOB DUTIES: Labor American converters. Carlson company

REASON FOR LEAVING:

DATES OF EMPLOYMENT: FROM: TO:	TOTAL TIME EMPLOYED: YEARS: MONTHS:	HOURS PER WEEK:	STARTING SALARY: $	FINAL SALARY: $

COMPANY NAME: Isanti Boys Ranch ②   **ADDRESS:** Phone # 444-5538   **SUPERVISOR:**

JOB TITLE:

YOUR JOB DUTIES: woodworking, lawn care, maintance ass. star Lumley instructor.

REASON FOR LEAVING:

DATES OF EMPLOYMENT: FROM: TO:	TOTAL TIME EMPLOYED: YEARS: MONTHS:	HOURS PER WEEK:	STARTING SALARY: $	FINAL SALARY: $

COMPANY NAME: **ADDRESS:**

JOB TITLE:

YOUR JOB DUTIES:

REASON FOR LEAVING:

DATES OF EMPLOYMENT: FROM: TO:

EXPLAIN ANY GAPS IN YOUR WORK HISTORY: In car...

Application 2

1. Are you working now .... ☒No ☐Yes - Hours per week: _____   Hourly Wage: _____
2. If married, is your spouse employed .. ☐No ☐Yes - Hours per week: _____   Hourly Wage: _____
3. If unemployed, did you receive a termination/layoff notice .... ☒No ☐Yes - Date received: _____
4. Unemployment compensation status .... ☐Eligible Claimant ☒Not Eligible ☐Claim Exhausted
5. Are you able to work: ☒Yes ☐No - If not, why _____
6. What have you been doing since your last job _Recuperating from bout with Spinal Miningitis_

LIST YOUR WORK EXPERIENCE COMPLETELY STARTING WITH YOUR PRESENT OR MOST RECENT JOB

COMPANY NAME: Good Food + Company   **ADDRESS:** 4920 Excelsior Blvd

JOB TITLE: Dishwasher/maintenance   **SUPERVISOR:** Gary Quam

YOUR JOB DUTIES: Misc. Cleaning, Table cleaning and Setting, along with Dishwashing. Also moping Floors, and vacuming Floors.

REASON FOR LEAVING: Quit (gave notice) To Look for something better.

DATES OF EMPLOYMENT: FROM Sept 1988 TO May 1990	TOTAL TIME EMPLOYED: YEARS 1 MONTHS 21	HOURS PER WEEK 40	STARTING SALARY: $4.25-HR.	FINAL SALARY: $4.75 HR.

COMPANY NAME: Fellowship manor   **ADDRESS:** 1201 Golden Gate ave, San Francisco, Calif.

JOB TITLE: Janitorial/maintenance   **SUPERVISOR:** Antoinette Commer

YOUR JOB DUTIES: Cleaned, moped, waxed and buffed Floors. Also did repair work, - Light Plumbing, and carpentey, and Lock replacement on unit doors.

REASON FOR LEAVING: Came back home To Minn. To help mom Take care of dad, who was Terminal.

DATES OF EMPLOYMENT: FROM Feb 1988 TO Jun 1988	TOTAL TIME EMPLOYED: YEARS MONTHS 4	HOURS PER WEEK 40	STARTING SALARY: $200. Wkly	FINAL SALARY: $Same

COMPANY NAME: Civic Center Hotel   **ADDRESS:** 11 street at Market San Francisco Calif.

JOB TITLE: Desk Clerk   **SUPERVISOR:** Gerda Kirchner/owner

YOUR JOB DUTIES: Registered + checked out guests, handled Rent money, made out daily Shift Reports, and operated Switchboard.

REASON FOR LEAVING: Laid off

DATES OF EMPLOYMENT: FROM Aug 1987 TO Jan 1988	TOTAL TIME EMPLOYED: YEARS MONTHS 5	HOURS PER WEEK 40	STARTING SALARY: $200 Wkly	FINAL SALARY: $Same

EXPLAIN ANY GAPS IN YOUR WORK HISTORY: Took 3 months off during Summer of 1988, To help my mom To nurse my dad, who was severely ill.

Which one of these two applications would you respond to if you were an employer?

Look over the two applications on the previous page. Who would you contact for an interview?

Now, create your own mistake-free application.

Your Master Application

PERSONAL INFORMATION:

First Name _____ Middle Name _____

Last Name _____

Street Address _____

City, State ZIP Code _____

Phone Number (___)_____

E-Mail Address _____

Are you eligible to work in the United States? Yes _____ No_____

If you are under age 18, do you have an employment/age certificate? Yes ___ No ___

Have you ever been in prison or jail? Yes_____ No_____

If yes, please explain: _____

_____

POSITION/AVAILABILITY:

Position Applied For _____

Days/Hours Available

Monday ____ Tuesday ____ Wednesday ____ Thursday ____ Friday ____

Saturday ____ Sunday ____

Hours Available: from _____ to _____
What date are you available to start work? _____

EDUCATION:

Name and Address of School - Degree/Diploma - Graduation Date

_____

_____

Skills and Qualifications: Licenses, Skills, Training, Awards

_____

_____

EMPLOYMENT HISTORY:

Present or Last Position:

Employer: _____

Address: _____

Supervisor: _____

Employer's Phone: _____ E-mail:_____

Your Position or Title: _____

From: _____ To: _____

Responsibilities: _____

_____

Salary: _____

Reason for Leaving: _____

Previous Position:

Employer: _____

Address:_____

Supervisor: _____

Employer's Phone: _____ E-mail:_____

Your Position or Title: _____

From: _____ To: _____

Responsibilities: _____

Salary: _____

Reason for Leaving: _____

May We Contact Your Present Employer? Yes _____ No _____

REFERENCES: (Name and Contact Information)

_____

_____

_____

I certify that information contained in this application is true and complete. I understand that false information may be grounds for not hiring me or for immediate termination of employment at any point in the future if I am hired. I authorize the verification of any or all information listed above.

Signature_____ Date_____

A CREATIVE WAY TO USE YOUR MASTER APPLICATION

An ex-offender was interested in working in sales at a retail store. He put together a mistake-free application, made several copies, and brought it to the local shopping mall. What made it different is that he attached a simple cover letter:

I recently came by to inquire about employment opportunities with your store, and left an application for you to review.

I welcome the opportunity to speak with you about available positions. Thank you.

Jose Smartlee, (234) 555-0202
josesmartlee@gmail.net

He used only a half-sheet of paper for the cover letter. He attached it to the application. It takes an average of twenty-to-thirty minutes to complete an application, even when using your mistake-free cheat sheet. Imagine how much ground you could cover with this approach.

Broaden your job search by applying to several retailers at once, such as those in a shopping mall. Photo by Dennis Mojado.

RESUMES

PURPOSE OF RESUMES
TYPES OF RESUMES

- BASIC RESUME
- OFFENDER LAYS IT ON THE LINE
- GRAPHICS
- SOMETHING FROM NOTHING

PURPOSE OF RESUMES

YOUR RESUME IS YOUR MARKETING TOOL

You need a good looking, accurate resume.

Customize your resume according to the job you are applying for and your personality.

Create a functional, or skills, resume. Leave off employment dates. You may want to design a resume with different fonts, sizes, and highlighting. Choose the design you would be most likely to pick if you were a hiring manager, and seek others' opinion, if possible.

It is a good idea to have two or three different types of resumes ready. Target them to the specific jobs for which you are applying. Look at each of the following sample resumes and at the resume at the start of this book on page 5. To get an edge, you need a resume that stands out.

RESUMES DON'T GET JOBS. THEY GET INTERVIEWS!

A resume is a one-page description of:

- What you could do for an employer
- Job duties/responsibilities
- Employment history
- Education

A resume is secondary to a well-written application.

Have you ever seen a negative resume?

5723 Haynes Court
Cleveland, OH 12345
Phone: (220) 987-6543
E-Mail: jmcseen@gmail.net

John McSeen

Job Objective	A position as a professional warehouse worker that displays my skills and abilities, which may lead to upper management in the future.

Work Experience 2004-2007   Grand Furniture   Cleveland, OH
Shop Repair
- Responsible for repairing broken or torn furniture
- Ensured products were shipped in and out of warehouse in an effective, timely manner
- Maintained accurate record of company accounts

2003-2004   Club 121   Sandusky, OH
Bar Back
- Responsible for all liquor in accordance with ABC regulations
- Ensured that bartender was fully stocked throughout the shift

2002-2003   Carpet Cleaner Company   Erie, OH
Carpet Cleaning Technician
- Ensured customers' carpets were cleaned and sanitized in accordance with company guidelines
- Managed coworkers to ensure chemicals were used properly
- Made sure team completed tasks on time

1998-1999   Lone Star Cantina   Erie, OH
Line Cook
- Excellent cook and hard worker
- Increased company revenue by selling accurately cooked steaks

Education 1994-1996   **Tall Wood High School**   Erie, OH
- High School Diploma

Interests I am an outgoing individual, a great communicator, and good with my hands. I am always looking to get the best out of life.

References *Professional references available upon request.*

Offender Lays It On the Line Resume

Gerald W. Goals
3122 Future Street
Great Lakes, MI 99102
Phone: (517) 123-4567 E-mail: gwgoals@yahoo.net

Objective	To obtain a challenging position in which I will learn new skills and trades that will enable me to stay competitive in the work force.
Experience	■ Answer telephones and interview people for vacant job openings ■ Supervise and train new employees, inventory sales and merchandise ■ Perform general office work to run a small business ■ Clean offices and kitchens and perform other janitorial work ■ Operate 855 John Deere tractor and maintain lawns ■ Complete projects with landscaping and building materials ■ Set up tables and chairs for meetings and graduations

Work History

October 2005 – May 2009 2918 Giblet's Lane, Great Lakes, MI	Chicken and More, Inc.
September 2000 – July 2002 3737 Rhodes Rd., Great Lakes, MI	Adult Achievers
April 1999 – July 2000 335 Toffee St., Great Lakes, MI	ACM Baked Goods
August 1998 – April 1999 3130 Foode Court, Great Lakes, MI	Pap's Café

Education 1994–1998 North High School Great Lakes, MI
Graduated 1998

Personal

I have been convicted of a felony for distribution of narcotics. I served seven months in the ICC (intensive confinement center) federal military boot camp. **This took courage** ☞

I have the ability to organize and schedule heavy workloads. I am a quick learner, especially in manual, hands-on trades, and possess good leadership skills. I can also lift over 100 pounds.

JOE BODYMAN
2727 Race Car Road
Speedway, USA 22334
(602) 555-4454
E-Mail: JoeBodyMan@yahoo.org

EMPLOYMENT GOALS:
To continue to develop my knowledge and skill as an auto body repair technician

WORK ETHIC:
Highly motivated, self-directed, meticulous, work well with co-workers

SKILLS:
Metal working, wire feed, gas brazing and cutting, painting and paint preparation, parts fabrication, and front-end alignment. Knowledge of standard and uni-body frame straightening systems. Working familiarity with snap tools. Background in automobile mechanics, automotive maintenance, troubleshooting, and repair.

WORK EXPERIENCE:
Two years' practical training at Brooklyn Technical College. Five years' working experience in family-owned auto repair shop in Cook, NY. Four months' experience in auto body repair, including paint prep work.

Tire Installer/Repairer
Reno Tire Warehouse
Mounted, balanced, and repaired tires, replaced batteries, and performed light mechanical duties.

Paint Preparer
Coach Craft Auto Body
Primed, sanded, buffed, removed trim, delivered, and picked up vehicles.

EDUCATION:
Brooklyn Technical College, Brooklyn, New York
Auto Body Repair

Ernie

Alley #3, Corner of Armitage and Damen, Chicago, IL 60626
(312) 569-2345
E purr@yahoo.org

OBJECTIVE
Long-term position as Housecat

QUALIFICATIONS
Proven stud potential
Highly developed purring mechanism
Excellent nonverbal communication skills
Omnivorous: Strong rodent-control capabilities
Affectionate. Adaptable. Rare feline willingness to follow established guidelines.

EXPERIENCE
BARNCAT, Westchester Estate, New York   2 years
Ensured day-to-day rodent and small animal control for two-story 35,000 square foot barn.
Consumed average of five rodents per day.
Achieved 37 percent reduction in barn swallow population.
Awarded feline leukemia inoculation after one month of service.
Earned in-house privileges for outstanding service and deportment after only two months on the job!

ALLEYCAT, Wilshire Blvd., Los Angeles, California   3 years
Successfully maintained territorial boundaries of four square block area in notoriously competitive and dangerous location. Developed high degree of proficiency in urban survival, hunting, and scavenging skills.
Honored by co-cats for consistent expertise in maneuvering safely and adroitly through heavy skateboard, auto and roller-skate traffic.
Known sire of at least seventy-seven feline litters over nine-month period.

EDUCATION
Certificate, Feline Deportment
TOM AND JERRY ASSOCIATES, Hollywood, California
(one-year intensive with Tom of famed Tom & Jerry)
High Honors

REFERENCES
Sylvester
Alley #7
Corner Franklin and Nicollet
Dallas, TX 77912
(616) 871-3031

Tweety
Alley #14
Corner Wabash and Randolph
Chicago, IL 60629
(312) 333-4445

Your Job Search
Start Now—
PRIOR TO YOUR RELEASE

BEGIN BY...

Targeting companies you may be interested in working for. Look through the:

- ✓ Yellow Pages
- ✓ Newspaper classifieds
- ✓ Have your family or a counselor provide you with the results of Internet job searches that list job openings. If they are willing, have them electronically answer the ads with material you prepare and they put into the computer.

Send them:

- ✓ Letter
- ✓ Application or resume
- ✓ Job-performance evaluations
- ✓ Photographs of your work
- ✓ References
- ✓ Self-addressed stamped envelope

What do you have to lose?

A SAMPLE LETTER FOR RESPONDING TO AN AD

Answer classified or help-wanted advertisements from the geographical area where you wish to be employed.

Your Address
City, State ZIP
Your E-mail Address
see 'E' notes to the form letter
Date

Employer's Name
Employer's Company
Employer's Address
City, State ZIP

Dear _____:

 I read your advertisement in the *see 'A' notes to the form letter on the next page*, and I am writing to you about the potential for employment with your company.

 I would like the opportunity to present my current resume and talk with you. My situation is unique. I am looking for an employer who is willing to give me a chance to prove myself and who will put my skills and talents to productive use.

 For the past two years, I have been employed with *see 'B' notes to the form letter*. While the situation is not what you might consider traditional, the typical elements of any employment situation are all there. I have completed training, when necessary, to bring my skills up to the level required by each job. I had regular evaluations with my superiors, and I received written performance assessments. I am required to be on time and to be courteous, responsible, and hard working, expectations you would have of any good employee.

 My strengths are *see 'C' notes to the form letter*. I am confident that I can be an asset to your organization.

 I will be available for interviews beginning on *see 'D' notes to the form letter*. In the meantime, I can be contacted by mail. For your convenience, I am enclosing a self-addressed stamped envelope for your reply. I appreciate your consideration.

 Thank you for your time.

Sincerely,
Your Signature
Your Name (printed)

FILLING IN THE FORM LETTER: A, B, C, D and E

A. If you have read an ad for the job, be sure to include the name of the publication where you saw the ad, and the date it appeared.

"I read your advertisement in the classified section of the *Minneapolis Star Tribune* on Sunday, February 11."

"I noticed your ad for a carpenter in the Sunday classified section of the *Boston Globe* on July 14."

B. Here you can indicate more about your present situation.

"For the past three years, I have been employed by the State of Michigan as a chef."

"For the past few months, I have been working as a computer technician at the Correctional Facility in Oak Park Heights."

C. Here is the area where you really get them interested. Tell employers what you are good at, what you like to do, and what your specialty is.

"My areas of strength are attention to detail and accuracy. I am often called on to look over the reports of co-workers to help them spot errors and make sure that the work is complete."

"I really like working with people. I seem to get along with all types of people and have a knack for dealing with them."

"I've always been good at sales. I am able to see what motivates people and have a talent for overcoming their objections."

D. Give the date you will actually be available to go to an interview. You will probably need to add a few days to your release date, just to allow time for arranging transportation, appropriate clothing, and other issues.

E. Have a friend or family member sign you up for a free E-mail account, but only if this individual will agree to check it until you are out. See page 82 for instructions on getting an E-mail account.

EX MARIJUANA KINGPIN NEEDS A JOB

The following is taken from the resume of Bruce Perlowin, who, during the early 1980s, was a marijuana smuggler based in California. Perlowin was paroled in January after serving nine years of a fifteen-year sentence for drug smuggling and income-tax evasion. After he was paroled, Perlowin distributed about thirty copies of his resume; in February, he was hired as the national sales manager of Rain Forest Products in Oakland.

"After nine years of prison, having lost all the money I illegally made, I am looking for a normal job. Trying to fill out a job application is somewhat preposterous under the circumstances, so I am submitting my resume for consideration to your firm.

A knack for organization and sophistication—are desirable qualities for someone working in a company with a progressive, creative, and entrepreneurial corporate culture.

I would be of invaluable assistance to a company needing an industrious, personable, and skilled individual. My background has given me an intimate grasp of managerial and leadership skills. I want to work for a progressive company that doesn't hold an individual's past against him, especially if his debt to society has been fully paid.

A last point to consider is that I never smuggled cocaine—only marijuana. I never used violence in any form, in all my years in business. And I don't use drugs or alcohol; they impair efficiency on the job. In my previous line of work, I couldn't afford that. Now, I am anxious to start a career as a productive member of the community. I thank you for your time and consideration."

A FOLLOW-UP LETTER
(WHICH MAKES IT SIMPLE FOR THE EMPLOYER TO RESPOND)

Recently, I wrote to you regarding employment opportunities with your company. I realize your schedule may be quite hectic and, similarly, my situation is unique.

I would appreciate it if you could complete the short form I have enclosed and return it in the self-addressed stamped envelope provided.

Thank you for your attention to this matter.

Your Signed Name
Your Printed Name

FROM: (Your name) _____

TO: _____

DATE: _____

   ❑   Please return to: (Your Name and Address)

   ❑   Please call me to schedule an interview.
        My number is _____

   ❑   Send me more information.

   ❑   Contact me upon release.

   ❑   We are not hiring now.

   ❑   Try this company: _____

Name_____ Title_____

Company _____

Address _____

City/State/Zip _____

Telephone _____

SELF-ADDRESSED STAMPED ENVELOPE

Any time you send a letter to an employer requesting a response, enclose a self-addressed stamped envelope.

Your Name
Address
City, State Zip

This will greatly increase your chances of a reply.

Send your correspondence on a *Tuesday* or a *Wednesday*. The mail is usually lighter near the end of the week, so you have a better chance of having your letter read.

FOLLOW UP

Any time you contact employers, by telephone, in person, or through e-mail ask them if you can schedule an interview at the time you fill out their application. The worst they can say is "no," and if they do say "yes," you save yourself an additional trip.

DO NOT WAIT FOR THE EMPLOYER TO CALL YOU!

If employers have not contacted you after seven days, contact them and say something like this:

"I recently completed an application for a position in your warehouse. Have you had an opportunity to review my application? Could I schedule an interview?"

NO PHONE? ONE OPTION

How is an employer going to contact you if you have no phone? Even before you apply to buy a cell phone, you should arrange to have a telephone through a voice-mail service. Companies provide you with a phone number, which you can give to a potential employer. Messages can be left at this number, and you can retrieve your messages from any phone. When employers call the number provided, it will ring once, then go to a recording. This service costs $8.95 and up per month. One provider is

American Voice Mail
2310 S. Sepulveda Blvd
Los Angeles, CA 90064
(800) 347-2861

You can also visit http://www.americanvoicemail.com for more information.

Many voice mail services will also provide fax-to-e-mail service. See page 82 to learn how to obtain a free E-mail address.

WHAT IS THE BEST WAY TO FIND A JOB?

✓ Through friends and acquaintances

✓ At churches or other houses of worship

✓ Newspapers

✓ Yellow Pages

✓ CraigsList

✓ Internet

✓ Your parole or probation officer

✓ Community bulletin boards

✓ School counseling offices

✓ Trade magazines

✓ Cold calling

✓ "Pounding the pavement"

✓ One-stop centers and unemployment offices

✓ Government agencies

✓ Community organizations

There is no one way to find a job: the best way is the way that finds you your job. A job search can consist of all these methods.

HEY MAN... WHERE ARE YOU WORKING?

Word of mouth can be your best job search tool! No matter where you are, ask others about job opportunities or placement services in your area.

In a halfway house, shelter, or in a church or other house of worship, you could ask people where they are currently working. Who knows? Someone could open the employment door for you, as well.

Also, find out from your case manager where previous ex-offenders have found work—he or she may have a list of potential employers.

This man is working as a carpenter–medieval style. With some creative hunting, there is no telling what work you will find. Photo: Wikimedia Commons.

CREATIVE JOB SEARCHES

Picasso

Before he was incarcerated, Warren was a master painter. Upon his release, he found some old paint clothes, went to the local paint store, and hung around waiting for painters to come and buy paint. He would approach them and ask if they needed help. It did not take him long to find a job. Sadly, he is now serving 12 months. He cannot stay away from the bottle.

Following Her Own Plan

Carla hired herself out as temp, calling large companies, offering her services, and taking $13.00 an hour. If she had worked through a temp agency, she would earn only $8.00 an hour.

You Provide the Mower—I'll Provide the Muscle

Sam, an ex-offender, did not even have a mower. He created an ad for his local newspaper that advertised: "You Provide the Mower—I'll Provide the Muscle." The ad cost about $25. He got many jobs—and established a client base that he services every two-to-three weeks.

Hanging Around

Sol, an ex-offender, went to a golf course and hung around the clubhouse, asking any golfers if they needed a caddie. Since some golfers are lazy, he got jobs, had a fun job, and no one asked him if he had a felony.

Another ex-offender, John, would go down to the golf course, roll up his jeans and collect golf balls that golfers hit into the water. Then, he would sell them to the clubhouse. He began to regularly strip down and dive for golf balls. Later, he decided to learn how to scuba dive and began collecting hundreds of balls at a time, which he would sell to wholesalers. This was in-between his stints in prison, and according to him, he made a handsome living from it.

Finding a job is like fishing. You keep throwing a line into the water hoping for a bite. It is similar to finding a job. You keep pounding on doors until you get a "yes."

POUNDING THE PAVEMENT

Ken, a parolee, lived in a tourist community. His parole officer suggested he go down to the boardwalk and apply to restaurants and hotels. He spent the day applying for jobs, and left with a job at a hotel with starting pay of $9.00 an hour.

TEMPORARY JOB SERVICES

After serving seven years, an ex-offender was released and registered at several temporary agencies. He was placed in a plumbing warehouse. After 450 hours on the job, he was hired by the company. After a year, he was placed in their apprenticeship program earning $16.00 an hour, with the potential to earn more as he learns more.

Your probation or parole officer may frown on working through a temp agency, because work may be sporadic, but it might be the quickest way to secure employment. After all, the temp agency does not make any money if they do not fill positions. A temp position also gives employers opportunities to evaluate your performance. Always ask the temp service if this is temp-to-hire or day labor.

Temporary work may lead to well-paid, skilled jobs.
Photo: Gunnery Sergeant R.L. Jaggard.

39

COMMON JOBS

The most common jobs secured by ex-offenders, whether just released or on probation, include:

1. Warehouse
2. Manufacturing
3. Construction
4. Hotel
5. Janitorial
6. Landscaping
7. Temp-to-hire positions, obtained by working with a temporary staffing agency
8. Phone sales (this may be a first job, and very short-lived)
9. Customer Service
10. Food service: there are more jobs in the restaurant industry (not just fast food) than any other field. There are a variety of positions, most with on-the-job training. One ex-offender was hired upon release as a prep cook at a chain restaurant, earning barely over minimum wage. Two years later, he was the restaurant's manager.

If you are sure-footed and not afraid of heights, become a roofer and reshingle a roof. U.S. Navy photo by Mass Communication Specialist Seaman Kelly E. Barnes.

GREEN JOBS

Our country is becoming more energy-efficient. As a result, jobs are being created in the green energy field and most of them offer on-the-job training. Retrofitting buildings for increased energy efficiency, expanding transit and freight rail, constructing efficient electrical grid systems, installing wind and solar power systems, and many other jobs are available in this growing sector.

YOU NEED TO WORK AT A TAX-PAYING JOB —

NOT A JOB WHERE YOU ARE PAID UNDER THE TABLE.

A job can transform you from a con to a vital part of your community.
Photo:Wikimedia Commons.

YOUR FIRST JOB

Your initial job is probably the most difficult one to obtain, but it is the most important one. The job sets the tone for future jobs that pay more. You need to stay on this, your first job, a minimum of six months.

By staying on the job for at least six months, you demonstrate that you are serious about changing your life, that you are an employee that your employer can count on, and you begin to build a positive work history. The longer you stay on the job, the further you distance yourself from your criminal record. Employers will still be hesitant to hire offenders. However, now that you have established a work history and have a positive recommendation from your past employer, your new potential employer will consider you more seriously.

Your success is in direct proportion to the effort you put forth!

YOU MAY NOT LIKE YOUR FIRST JOB, BUT IT IS ONE YOU NEED

Sometimes, you have just one thing to trade for money: your hard work.
Photo by Ben Aveling.

- It was the hottest time of the year—July. He was gathering carts from a hot, humid grocery store parking lot and bringing them back to the store. Within a few months he was transferred to the deli counter, which was air-conditioned.

- Her first job was at an animal kennel, cleaning cages. It does not get much lower than that! But it was more than a job to her: she found that her interest lay in working with animals, and she has been promoted to kennel manager.

- She is very bright, but also an ex-offender. She is a member of Mensa, an organization for people with very high IQs. She has a degree in aerospace engineering. Her first job? She worked behind the counter at a hole-in-the-wall hot dog joint.

INCENTIVES FOR EMPLOYEES

1. FEDERAL BONDING PROGRAM

Ex-offenders, persons with a history of alcohol or drug abuse, individuals with poor credit records, and high-risk job applicants are frequently rejected for employment because of their backgrounds. At an interview, one helpful thing you can do is tell your prospective employer about the Federal Bonding Program.

The Federal Bonding Program is a business insurance policy that protects an employer in case there is a loss of money or property due to an employee's dishonesty. This bond covers the employer for $5,000, with no deductible for the employer, if the job for which you are being bonded is full-time work. Employers are able to protect their assets at no charge, and this policy is good for up to six months. After six months, an employer can purchase more coverage from the McLaughlin Company in Washington, DC.

For an application or further information, call or write to: (800) 223-2258. Applications are also available at your state Job Service Office.

Federal Bonding Program
1725 DeSales St. NW, Suite 700
Washington, DC 20036

2. EMPLOYEE-TARGETED TAX CREDIT PROGRAM

The Work Opportunity Tax Credit (WOTC), authorized by the Small Business Jobs Protections Act, is a federal tax credit that encourages employers to hire targeted groups of job seekers—including ex-offenders—by reducing employers' federal income tax liability by as much as $2,400 per qualified new employee.

For an application, call (800) 829-1040 or visit www.irs.ustreas.gov

THE QUESTION

A REAL ANSWER TO A TOUGH QUESTION:

"HAVE YOU EVER BEEN IMPRISONED OR JAILED?"

HOW ARE YOU GOING TO RESPOND?

Terry Smyth reported to his probation officer: "I was just fired from my job."

The probation officer asked: "What happened?"

Terry answered: "I wrote 'No' on the felony question. They did a background check and I was kicked to the curb. If I answered 'yes', they would not hire me. If I lie, they will fire me."

The common consensus by counselors, including this author, is to check "yes" and write "will explain in interview." One ex-offender wrote: "I am an ex-offender. Do you believe in second chances?" Yet, there is a lot of disagreement among felons and employers on how to handle it. However, employers agree on this—they want an honest response—do not lie.

The following are common responses from employers:

- I consider applicants on a case-by-case basis.

- I want to know upfront what their conviction is. That way, I will not waste my time or theirs.

- I'd rather be short-handed than hire an ex-offender.

- I have had a bit of trouble with the law and am a recovering alcoholic, so I look at applicants differently and am willing to give them a chance if they express sincerity and motivation.

Be prepared for rejections due to your record. However, it is a numbers game and eventually you will get that one "yes."

Use the space with that question to sell yourself! Highlight the positives! The next page shows how to do this.

HIGHLIGHTING THE POSITIVES

Referring to the common response, one employer stated, "I do not like that answer. It makes me wonder if there is more to it than they are willing to discuss." Other employers do not mind if you put down, "will discuss in the interview." However, be prepared to talk about it.

One of the best explanations:

After his release, Marcus M. described how he was going to explain his felony:

"Four years ago I assaulted someone at a party while I was drinking. I used very poor judgment. While incarcerated, I used my time for education, and completed three years of college. I also worked as a tutor in an adult basic education class and attended chemical dependency classes."

Marcus acknowledged his mistake and illustrated ways he had changed his behavior and life.

This is the time to take out your portfolio and show it to the interviewer!

To be believable, you have to put this in your own words!

LEAVING A JOB: THE NUMBER ONE PROBLEM

The number one problem is, and always has been, keeping your job once you have it. Why would you walk off the job during your shift? Why would you decide not to show up? Ask yourself those questions before you walk off your job. When you leave a job without telling anyone—without notice—common sense does not come into play. It happens all the time—and all it does is make it more difficult for you to get another job.

If you do not like your job, and feel you cannot take it another day, approach your supervisor and explain to her or him that this job is not working out for you, and that you plan to look for another position. Ask how much notice he or she would like. Your work history, even if it is only one day on the job, is a permanent record on your Social Security work history. Employers have access to this information about you. Standard notice is two weeks, but more than likely, they will tell you to finish out the day.

This way, you are not burning a bridge, and if your next employer calls to obtain a reference, your former employer can say you gave notice and you were not fired.

I urge you to consider this: it is always, always in your best interest not to leave a job until you have secured another job first!

DO NOT RUIN IT FOR OTHERS

You may not like your job, but by leaving on a positive note, you may give someone else an opportunity.

DON'T EVER LEAVE YOUR JOB WITHOUT HAVING ANOTHER JOB LINED UP.

YOUR IMAGE

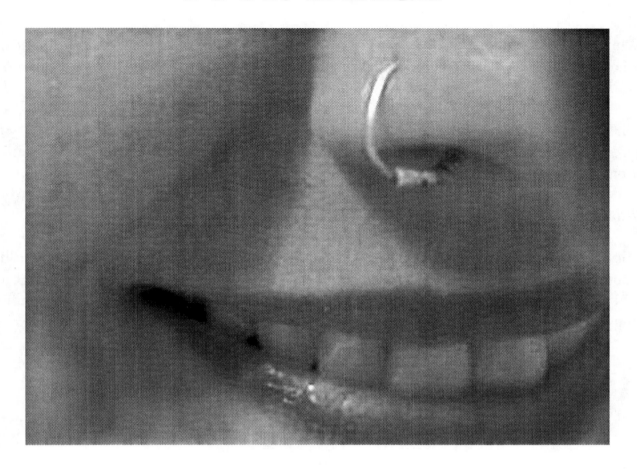

WHAT IMPRESSION DO YOU MAKE?

While at a conference, I saw five men sitting at a table. Four of them had on suits and ties, and were clean shaven and well groomed. Who are these guys? They looked like they came out of *GQ Magazine* and worked for a Fortune 500 company.

Turns out all five of them were on parole. One of the men had been released only a few days prior to the conference. The fifth man had on jeans, a raggedy shirt, a long beard, and had long, straggly hair. He looked like he just came out of the "hole."

What type of impression do you think these gentlemen would make at an interview?

You do not have to wear a suit and tie every day, but your appearance and how you dress does make an impression. Dress and look your best at all times, not just at the interview but when filling out applications, visiting social services organizations, and so forth. You never know who is watching you.

Wear a long-sleeve shirt to cover your tattoos.

HOW DO YOU SOUND TO AN EMPLOYER?

You have every right to answer the phone any way you want, but what if it is an employer, calling to offer you a job? The message you have on your phone or voice mail can mean the difference in whether or not you get called for an interview. Many times, this author attempted to contact the clients he supervises, and when he does (that is, when their phone is in service and has paid minutes), he hears such things as:

"Yo, bro, you know the routine, so do it and you might hear back from me."

"What's up, speak, hey, you know what to do and when to do it."

The most annoying message is two to five minutes of obscene rap music. Do you think an employer has time to listen to that?

Then there are the cutesy messages. For example: "Thank you for calling Bad Bruce's Pizza Kitchen. Leave your order at the beep with your number."

This is not how you win over a prospective employer. Therefore, until you secure a job, you may want to consider a more appropriate and professional message. Try the following: "Hi, you have reached Bob Smith. I am not available at the moment. However, if you leave your name and telephone number, I will get back to you as soon as I am able."

This type of message is more likely to entice a future employer to leave his or her name and call-back information. Professional manners, in this case, are your first impression, and you definitely want to leave a good one.

What kind of an impression are you making? You can practice making a good impression while you are still behind bars.

AN INTERVIEW

Congratulations! You have used your time and resources wisely and you just got a call back for an interview. Now what?

EMPLOYERS SPEAK OUT

This information came directly from employers!

"Don't say you'll take any job!"

"I want to know if you have a plan for your life and future."

"I must see interest and enthusiasm. Are you there because you want to be, or did your PO tell you to get a job?"

"If you are snotty or rude to my receptionist, no matter how well you do in the interview, you will not get the job."

"I want to hear that applicants will be available for every shift that they are scheduled for, and will not walk out during their shift if they become angry or if something doesn't go right."

EMPLOYERS' EXPECTATIONS

"I can teach an employee just about anything about the job but honesty."

1. **Be on time.** If your shift begins at 8 A.M. you are expected to be at your work station by 8 A.M., ready to work. No walking through the door at 8 A.M.!

2. **Have good attendance.** Why is it that most employees call in sick on Mondays? Because of this, some employers have even had to move payday to Monday. Attendance has improved!

3. **Follow instructions.** You will have a supervisor who has more experience and training than you do. You are expected to follow his or her instructions.

4. **No cell phones turned on:** not even on your hip.

5. **Got tattoos?** If you have visible tattoos, you may be required to wear a long-sleeved shirt to cover them.

6. **Employers are taking a risk in hiring you.** So, do not complain or whine about the job. You have a job, and you will be paid to perform work.

Your Image

I'LL TAKE ANYTHING!

This is a common response when ex-offenders are first out on the street. A few days or weeks later, however, they have left that job due to *job incompatibility*. Think about the proper job fit for you. As long as you are looking for work, why not look for a job you may like?

Work at a job that fits you, rather than one you think you can fit into; otherwise, one day you will decide to give up the job. Of course, your first job is a stepping-stone to something better. Along the way, you are establishing a current job history.

Make the effort to find a job that fits you.

DOES THE RIGHT JOB MAKE A DIFFERENCE?

Between the ages of seventeen and twenty-one, Charles had jobs in restaurants, retail stores, grocery stores, landscaping, and other fields too numerous to list. All those jobs had one thing in common: *he was fired from all of them!*

Now, Charles has an entry-level position as a *"professional gopher"* in a political organization. What makes this job different? His passion is politics. He is always on time, never calls in sick, and continuously talks about his job.

Tell *him* the right job does not make a difference!

55

YOU ARE A ROLE MODEL

Plan for how you will support your family both economically and emotionally.

DANGEROUS,
NON-TRADITIONAL JOBS

Keep things interesting: learn to operate heavy, mobile machinery like this truck-mounted drill rig! Beware of blow-back. Become a roughneck.
Photo: Wikimedia Commons.

DANGEROUS, TOUGH NON-TRADITIONAL JOBS

A young man in his twenties pushed his hang glider off a cliff, failed to catch an updraft, and slammed to the ground 600 feet below. He was near death and in intensive care for a long time. After months of therapy, he finally recovered and went home. The next day, he went hang gliding.

No ex-offender has ever come into my office requesting an office job. However, ex-offenders want to know how to become a **professional skateboarder**, a **race car driver**, or a recruit for the **merchant marine**, or a **poker player**.

Many ex-offenders do not have the interest or desire to work in mainstream society. Instead, they tend to prefer jobs that are exciting, risky, dangerous, and adventurous. The following pages contain a list of possible jobs that may be right for you. Most do not require formal education. You can learn on the job, or complete a short training program. Try not to kill yourself.

Photo: U.S. Fish and Wildlife Service.

Logger: Work in-out-of-the-way places for long hours, climbing trees, cutting them down, getting logs downhill and loading them onto trucks or into narrow canals of water. Anyone in the way could end up dead.

Ultimate Fighter: If you liked barroom brawling, then this might be the job for you. Here you train and fight for cash, much as boxers and wrestlers do. As an ultimate fighter, there are no rules. Last one standing wins the prize.

MORE NON-TRADITIONAL JOBS

Snake Wrangler: You must have nerves of steel for this position. You get to care for the deadliest snakes in the world and extract their venom to be made into antidotes for snakebites. The danger is in the extraction. You have to be able to charm these dangerous reptiles, so you can steal their venom without it going into you.

High-Altitude Plumber: If you have a fear of heights, you won't like this job. You must be able to climb some of the highest buildings in the world, carrying all your equipment on your body, to fix things no one else will even go near. At least it pays well. But watch that first step—it's a killer.

Pit Crew: It's one thing to drive a car, and a different and dangerous thing to be part of the four-to-five person team that has to work together to make sure that in seconds, the car gets back out there in the race with a chance to win. In those seconds, disaster could strike any of the team as they are changing tires or hot engine parts. In this fast, furious, beat-the-clock position, you have to be a team player.

Exotic Animal Trainer: Do you like animals? If so, this job could be for you. It is very dangerous—these aren't house cats we are talking about. As an exotic animal trainer, you will be in a large cage with lions, tigers, bears, or animals large enough to crush you with one foot. Your only protection is a whip and a chair to hide behind. Nothing causes the adrenaline to pump through your body like being charged by an angry tiger that weighs more than you and is likely hungry. There's nothing docile about these animals,. With persistence and courage, you might find them wrapped around your little finger—or that may be all that's left of you.

Bike Messenger: If you live in a major city and are in great shape, you might enjoy this job. As a bicycle messenger, you have to be able to get places faster than the traffic and pedestrians are moving. Sometimes you are moving against traffic, and any of these deliveries could mean your death, because traffic does not watch out for you. Make sure your brakes are working; hellish hills and curves may catch you unaware as well.

Alligator Wrangler: You must have strength, fortitude and cunning to out-maneuver these reptiles. They drag their dinner underwater, and then save it to eat later. Bring the alligator under control, but watch those jaws. They will take any part of you that they can. Just think of Captain Hook from *Peter Pan*. Yeah.

Video Game Tester: If you like to remain stationary for long periods of time, this job is for you. The danger is in the number of calluses on your fingers and a loosening of the jaw muscles as your brain turns to mush. This is not for the faint of heart.

Slaughterhouse Worker: You have to have an iron stomach for this, and lack a sense of smell. You will be required to pick out the animals that get to die that day, then become the executioner. The danger? Some animals will fight to survive, and you might get bashed up against the stalls, escaping, if you are lucky, with a few broken bones.

Stuntman/Stuntwoman: If you like to live dangerously, would jump off a high-rise building with only an air mattress to break your ten-story fall, have no problem jumping out of a perfectly good airplane with only an emergency parachute, do not mind getting hit by a car, shot, stabbed, pushed down a flight of stairs, or set on fire, then this is your big break! You might have a history of doing some of this stuff already. Get paid to do what movie actors won't, but don't expect any thanks or invitations to red carpet events.

If you live long enough to be noticed, you might get invited to an actual Hollywood party. Just keep your nose clean. You don't want to end up back inside.

MORE NON-TRADITIONAL JOBS

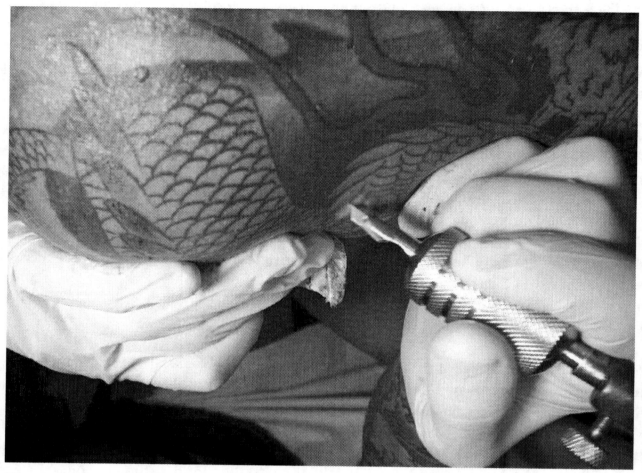

Photo: Michael Deschenes.

Tattoo Artist: Chances are, you got a couple of tattoos while you were inside, so you know how it feels. To do it legitimately, you must use sterile needles, clean ink, and have a high degree of artistic talent. No, you cannot slap anyone if they whine. This position takes loads of patience, and the ability to sit for long periods of time as you leave your permanent mark on people's bodies. The money is pretty good, and no one cares about your outward appearance. The more body art you display, the better your business. They don't have to know you got your tattos in prison.

Locksmith: This exciting activity may be listed on your rap sheet, but you can do it legally. It does require that you be licensed, so the cops can visit you first if something goes missing from a car or home you have unlocked. For most people, learning this trade takes time, but if you have the skills already, and like the adrenaline that flows through your body when you break in, there is good money in doing it legally. You will have to lose the "sticky fingers," though!

Cartoonist: If graffiti is one of the things that landed you in jail, if you learned to draw on smaller media, such as paper napkins, while inside, if you have a decent imagination (to create likeable characters, witty dialog, and silly stuff), and you are the patient type, you could earn good money if you are signed by a national publisher. This is a very positive, yet passive position, and it is work you can do from home.

Deep Sea Fisher: If you think you would like adventure on the high seas, heave ho, mate, and come aboard. You have to have an iron stomach for times when waves threaten to capsize your small fishing boat. You also have to like being wet for eighteen hours a day as you set about playing tug of war with the strongest fish in the sea. Often away from home for days, even weeks, at a time, there are no showers and you can't let the smell of your fellow anglers get in the way of potential hard cash. Did I mention the boat was small? Can't have a problem with claustrophobia either.

Photo credit: U.S. Fish and Wildlife Service

Non-Traditional Jobs

MORE NON-TRADITIONAL JOBS

Photo: Christophe Meneboeuf.

Coal Miner: Hope you're not claustrophobic. Here, you are lowered hundreds of feet into the ground to extract coal from shored-up dirt walls that could fall in and trap you underground with no light, food, water, or air. Toxic gases are always a hazard for workers, and if you survive, your retirement will be miserable — your lungs may give out on you due to the coal dust you inhaled. Not a pretty picture.

Structural Steel and Iron Worker: For this position, you must work many hundreds of feet above the ground. You must have good-balance sufficient to walk on beams of iron or steel only about as wide as your boot. Oh, and these beams are moving: crane operators often swing you and the beam into the appropriate position so you can weld one beam to another, not unlike a giant erector set. Due to the nature of the work and the danger of falls, the pay is usually very good. If you have a fear of heights, working in bad weather bothers you, or you can't make heads or tails of a bunch of lines on a paper (a blueprint), then this job is not for you.

Repossession Man or Woman: This legal job involves the same skills and nerve you had when you did it and got put in jail for your efforts. If you like to sneak onto people's property and steal their vehicles, you are welcome here! Be prepared to get shot at, yelled at, and hit with various objects as you give people a piece of paper that says you have the legal right to steal their car. That's not going to make them any nicer, so the quicker you are about it, the better. Bet you didn't think there was a legitimate version of your illegal activities.

Professional Skateboarder: If, for some reason, you think you haven't aged while on the inside, and therefore have the same balance and agility as you used to, try this profession. To be considered a pro at this extremely dangerous sport, you must balance on a two- or three-foot-long, by one-foot-wide, board with four small wheels beneath. Not only do you have to be able to stand on it, you have to make it move, and balance it uphill and downhill. That's not all. There are a lot of tricks you need to master, preferably on concrete courses made for the purpose. Be warned, this job causes ultimate road rage, and often broken bones, before you earn any money at all.

Musician: If you have been gifted like Mozart or Beyoncé, and you enjoy being free from most entanglements, such as a house, family, or normal job, this position might be for you. Not to shatter your dreams, but you might do better on the side streets of San Francisco, with a boom box, playing the instrument of your choice, hat on the ground to catch appreciation coins. Every once in a great while, there is an opening in a real band. This job requires diligence, and the rewards may be nothing more than the smiles from the crowd around you.

Smokejumper: This involves riding in a large airplane and getting dumped into the middle, most dangerous part of a wildfire with only a shovel, a breathing apparatus, and a somewhat protective uniform. You have to be able to read a map and have a good sense of direction to fight some of the meanest, hottest fires and still have an escape route. Hazard pay is about all you can expect, but it does get the blood pumping.

Pro Wrestler: You may have already learned some of the skills necessary for this "kick butt" profession. You must have a degree of acting ability for this one, too! Gymnastics is another useful skill here, as you are continually thrown into the ropes, picked up, and body slammed into the floor. Anger management with a licensed professional is a requirement for the duration of this very lucrative, yet primitive, job. The money can be good, if you can follow directions, and if you can humble yourself enough to take a fall now and then.

MORE NON-TRADITIONAL JOBS

Actor: If you can read this, have a decent memory, and like to dress up and be someone other than who you are, this position might fit you to a tee. There is money to be had in this industry, but you have to start at the bottom and work your way up, playing characters that are... well, like you, when they put you behind bars. Good luck!

Race Car Driver: If you enjoyed high speed chases on highways, this may be your niche. Does speed make the blood pump harder in your veins? Does the sound of an engine as it whines, topping out at 250 miles per hour, turn you on? If you learned in prison to react with lightning fast accuracy, and you answered yes to both questions, you could make a go of it. Ruthlessness is the key to good money in this back-stabbing profession. Right up your alley, huh?

If you have no education, no GED, and no diploma of any kind, any one of these positions is open to you. Usually, there is very little on-the-job training involved, so you must be a self-starter.

ADVENTUROUS, DANGEROUS, NON-TRADITIONAL JOB CONTACTS

BULLRIDER
Professional Rodeo Cowboys' Association
101 ProRodeo Dr
Colorado Springs, CO 80919
(719) 593-8840
www.prorodeo.com

CARTOONIST
National Cartoonists Society
Columbus Circle Station
New York, NY 10023
(212) 627-1550
www.reuben.org

COMMERCIAL DRIVER
www.dmv.org/cdl_education.php

COWBOY/COWGIRL
www.indeed.com/q-cowboy-jobs.html

ELECTRIC COMPANY LINEPERSON
Communications Workers of America
501 3rd St., NW
Washington, DC 20005
(202) 434-1100
www.cwa-union.org/jobs/

HIGH RISE WINDOW WASHER
International Window Cleaners of America
400 Admiral Blvd.
Kansas City, MO 64102
(816) 471-4922
www.iwca.org

LOBSTERMAN/LOBSTERWOMAN
The Lobster Conservancy
PO Box 235
Friendship, ME 04547
(207) 832-8224
www.lobsters.org/misc/contact.html

LOGGER
American Loggers Council
PO Box 2109
Cleveland, TX 77328
(281) 432-7167
www.americanloggers.org

MERCHANT MARINE
Marine Administrator
Seafarers International Union
5201 Auth Way
Camp Springs, MD 20746
(301) 889-0675
www.seafarers.org/jobs/

PROFESSIONAL WRESTLER
Florida Championship Wrestling
4535 South Pale
Pale, Florida 33611
www.flwrestling.com

This school is an official development territory of World Wrestling Entertainment.

RACECAR DRIVER
National Association for Stock Car and Auto Racing
1801 W. International Speedway Blvd.
Daytona Beach, FL 32114
(904) 253-0611
www.nascar.com Enter word jobs in the search engine on site.

REPOSSESSOR
American Recovery Association
PO Box 6788
New Orleans, LA 20124
(504) 367-0711
www.repo.org

STUNTPERSON
Stuntmen's Association of Motion Pictures
4810 Whitsett Ave.
North Hollywood, CA 91607
(818) 766-4334
http://www.stuntmen.com

BOOK
Careers for Nonconformists: A Practical Guide to Finding and Developing a Career Outside the Mainstream, by Sandra Gurvis. (Cambridge, Massachusetts: Da Capo Press, 1999.) The author discusses 75 nontraditional, creative, off-the-wall jobs. Break into a new field, survive, and thrive.

ENTREPRENEURS

DO YOUR OWN THING!

BE YOUR OWN BOSS!

This man, once a parolee, is now a successful businessman with his own business.

BE AN ENTREPRENEUR!

NOBODY'S GOING TO ASK IF YOU'RE A FELON

Starting a business sounds simple, doesn't it? Well, it is.

Running and growing a business is difficult!

Entrepreneurs are highly motivated self-starters. As an entrepreneur, you are responsible for all aspects of your job: bookkeeping, taxes, marketing, customer service, compliance with local laws and ordinances, licenses, inspections, and much more.

If starting your own business still sounds appealing, read on!

Ready to start out on your own? Think creatively! Provide a service no one else does.

Regardless of your background, education, or income, you could be an entrepreneur.

FACT: Wally Amos, a high school dropout, built a cookie empire.

FACT: Colonel Sanders was turned down by sixty-eight restaurants before starting Kentucky Fried Chicken.

FACT: Ben Cohen and Jerry Greenfield of Ben and Jerry's Ice Cream started their business after taking a correspondence course on how to make ice cream.

American Chopper is a popular cable TV show in prisons. As a welder by trade, Paul Teutel Sr. started a motorcycle business in his basement. In less than ten years, his custom-made choppers are known worldwide.

There are numerous stories like these—individuals start from nothing and with little or no money build companies and products that are known across the nation and even worldwide.

ENTREPRENEURS LIKE YOU

- A former inmate with a knack for painting printed up flyers, posted them around his new neighborhood, and was soon in business for himself.

- Within a year of his release, another man who started out with a hand mower had purchased a truck, had a custom sign made, and expanded his services to become Gentle Ben's Lawn Service.

- One woman began her post-incarceration life by working in a specialty fish store. She became fascinated by the variety, colors, shapes, and sizes of fish. Part of her job duties was to clean the fish tanks—not the most pleasant of jobs. She became proficient at it, however, and started a part-time business cleaning fish tanks in people's homes. She continues to work at the fish store, which provides a steady paycheck, as she builds her clientele.

- One entrepreneurial parolee started with $100.00. He bought perfume and cologne from a wholesale company. He went from shop to shop selling his goods. All was well—until he was fined $500.00 for working without a business license. It pays to do your homework *before* venturing out on your own!

- Fresh out of prison, Santana started a business called "Errands on the Run." She placed an ad in a small neighborhood newspaper offering her services. Grocery shopping, drop off and pick up dry cleaning, coffee delivery, and so on; she turned this small business into a full-time job.

- One young man was in a flooring store with his mother and overheard a customer ask an employee if he knew anyone who needed a job. So, the young man approached the customer. He did not have any experience, but learned how to lay carpet and install flooring. His entrepreneurial spirit will help him with his future business-ownership plans.

MORE ENTREPRENEURS

- Jeff served fifteen years and was living at his brother's house. One day he noticed a couple of guys going in and out of a house, with sheetrock and tools. He walked up to them and said, "Hey, you guys need help?" He was put to work for the day. At the end of the day, the foreman said, "I have a lot of work renovating houses, I'll give you a week's try." After 18 months, he is still working the same job. He showed entrepreneurial spirit. Down the road he is planning to start his own company.

- As a teenager, he worked for a pool installation and repair company. He went to prison, but once he was released, he started his own company. This will be hard to believe, but he now is making more than $100,000 a year. I have seen his tax returns.

Follow Your Passion

One probationer, Henry, worked as a mortgage broker–until the housing market collapsed. Fortunately, his wife had a full time job; but they were still struggling. He is a good pool player, making a few dollars here and there. He is currently developing his business plan, which includes opening a small billiards parlor.

There are many success stories of ex-offenders who have gone into business for themselves, but this is probably not something that will happen for you as soon as you are out of prison. The best way to start a business of your own is by moonlighting. Once you have secured a steady, legitimate job, start your own business in the evenings and on weekends. Continue to work your day job until you establish a solid customer base, and income from your business is double your income from your day job.

EX-CON BECOMES ENTREPRENEUR!

Dave* has battled with alcoholism, had scrapes with police, and struggled with his own learning problems. But those battles have not kept him from becoming his own boss. With the help of his wife, Dave has put his energies into building a small, growing upholstery business. For thousands of people who dream about going into business for themselves, Dave could be an inspiration.

"Here's a guy who, when we first met, was by all definitions a loser," said a college small business management instructor who lent Dave assistance. "He was obviously very savvy, but he brought all of this incredible baggage." Dave is a recovering alcoholic. He has been in prison. He has had problems reading and writing. And when it comes to applying for credit, "the fact that he's a minority doesn't help him one bit," the instructor said.

But with some management advice, a loan from his state's Department of Vocational Rehabilitation, and his own hard work, Dave has realized a dream. "I give a quality upholstery job for a fair price, and the work is coming in."

He advertises in the *Yellow Pages*, and finds customers by word of mouth. He charges $170 for labor, plus fabric costs, to upholster a chair, offers free pick-up, delivery, and in-home estimates, and has two employees. He grosses less than $100,000 a year. Dave says his target market is the working class and the "super rich."

He envisions expanding his business to manufacture custom sofas and chairs, so that clients could come in, pick out a frame, and select the fabric for their furniture. Dave would employ hard-to-hire employees, giving them training and building their confidence while they crafted a product. "Something has got to be done . . . to give our people some kind of skills," he said. "The difference between what we would be doing and what a trade school does is the school teaches fundamentals. No matter how much instruction you've had and [how many] books you've read, you need the hands-on experience and repetition to be able to get in there and feel comfortable cutting and working with the fabric."

"We'll be training the unskilled and giving them the skills, knowledge, and self-esteem, and they will make some kind of living wage. That's a personal goal of mine."

(Adapted from the Minneapolis Star-Tribune)

*Not his real name.

RESOURCES FOR ENTREPRENEURIAL EX-OFFENDERS

✓ Lindahl, Nicole and Debbie Mukamal, *2007. Venturing Beyond the Gates: Facilitating Successful Reentry with Entrepreneurship*, New York: John Jay College of Criminal Justice, Prisoner Reentry Institute. This booklet lists sources of funding and support for formerly incarcerated entrepreneurs and provides many examples of successful ex-offenders.
http: www.jjay.cuny.educentersinstitutes/pri/pri.ask
You can download it for free.

✓ Adams' *Businesses That You Can Start Almanac*, 2nd edition. 2006. Order from www.adamsmediastore.com. It lists businesses that you can start from under $1,000 and up. It is a great source for ideas.

✓ Another excellent resource for entrepreneurs is *Entrepreneur Magazine*. Your local library should have a copy of this monthly publication. If you would like your own subscription, sign up online at www.entrepreneur.com or contact:

Entrepreneur Magazine
Subscription Department
PO Box 55809
Boulder, CO 80323-5809

At the time of publication, one year, 12 issues, cost $11.97. Not a bad investment of one dollar per month. This company also publishes numerous how-to books that may help you start a variety of businesses.

✓ You also may enjoy *Think Outside the Cell: An Entrepreneur's Guide for the Incarcerated and Formerly Incarcerated*, by Joseph Robinson (2007), available at www.thinkoutsidethe-cell.com.

✓ The U.S. Small Business Administration (www.sba.gov) offers financial assistance and local resources.

Additionally, you may want to contact your local chamber of commerce or business administration. Retired entrepreneurs counsel potential entrepreneurs through the ins and outs of starting a small business. This service is free through mentor-matching organizations such as SCORE (www.score.org).

SPECIAL CONCERNS FOR WOMEN EX-OFFENDERS

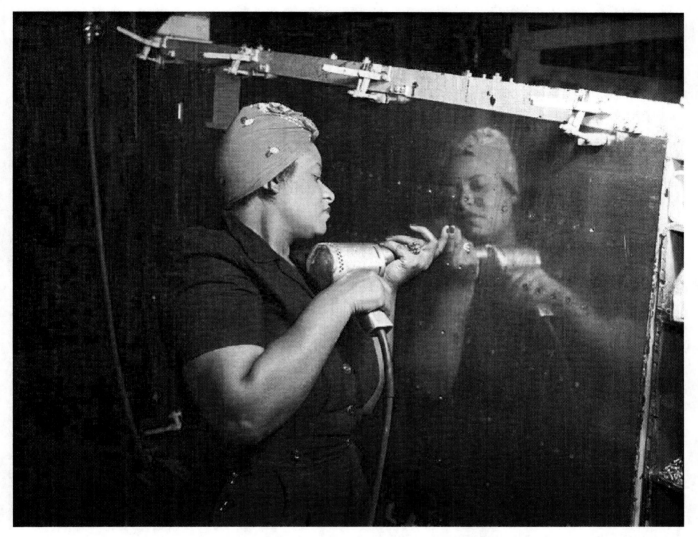

Women who find non-traditional employment often earn more than women in traditional jobs. Photo: Alfred T. Palmer, U.S. Office of War Information.

WOMEN EX-OFFENDERS' UNIQUE CHALLENGES

Women face some of the same issues as men when leaving prison, but many of their needs and challenges are unique. Most women who have been incarcerated have families to support. The majority of these women were incarcerated for a drug-related offense.

You know the challenges ahead. How are you going to face them? Create a plan. How are you going to take care of yourself and your children when you are released? Do you have access to education, substance-abuse treatment programs, or a parenting program on the inside? What resources can you access to help you with childcare, mental and physical health care, and substance abuse? Take advantage of these. Build a strong set of tools you can take with you when you rejoin the community.

I supervise several women. Some are struggling day by day, but continue to persist in building a new life for themselves; others have given up all hope, and may return to drugs and prison. Here are some of their stories.

One woman was released from custody late on Friday afternoon. She reported to the probation and parole office the following Monday morning, holding the classified section of the Sunday newspaper. "I have two interviews this afternoon," she said. Later that day, she called to say she had found a job at $9.00 an hour. She lives with a relative, and her mother has custody of her son. This former inmate plans to go to school and become a social worker for juveniles.

After three stints in prison, the last for seven years, one woman has been on the streets for eighteen months. She secured a job, moved in with her father, reunited with her children, and saw her grandchildren for the first time. Things are starting to turn around for her! She has remained drug free, recently got married, and now shares an apartment with her husband.

Another twenty-three-year-old ex-offender has four children, and after a year of living with her aunt, she is now in a shelter. She has maintained a steady job, however, and plans to move into an apartment. Once her situation is stable, she intends to attend cosmetology school. She has never, ever given up.

All of these women have one thing in common: they have jobs, even if they do not make a great wage, and they are beginning to create independent lives for themselves, even if they are not living independently. They plan to stick with their jobs until they can obtain better-paying, more satisfying work. To advance in life on the outside, both you and they need to get better jobs. How do you get better jobs? You get better jobs by educating yourself. Many non-traditional jobs pay more than the usual jobs women get. Learn to be a veterinary technician, a heavy equipment operator, a chef, a social worker, a hair stylist, an electrician. If you want to become self-sufficient and live on your own, you must take this step. Remember: *learn more, earn more!*

RESOURCES FOR WOMEN

Support is available to women leaving incarceration. Whether you have a criminal record and need a job, or are moving from welfare to work, several organizations are sensitive to your particular needs. Some resources follow.

Housing

For immediate housing needs, use 211, First Call for Help, to find resources in your area. If you are looking for a long-term, stable home or apartment, visit the Office of Housing and Urban Development (HUD) on the Internet. HUD's Bookshelf pages at http://www.hud.gov/library/index.cfm puts all their most popular and important resources in one place for you.

Food, if you are pregnant or the mother of young children

- For help meeting your basic nutritional needs, contact your WIC state agency. Type WIC and the name of your state into an Internet search engine.

Help on the Outside

- National Domestic Violence Hotline: 1-800-799-SAFE or 1-800-787-3224 (TTY)

- Rape, Abuse, and Incest National Network (RAINN): 1-800-656-HOPE

Mentors

- Visit the National Association of Women Business Owners (NAWBO), on the Internet at http://dev.nawbo.org/section_29.cfm for a listing of business resources, articles, and more.

- The African American Women's Organization/National Council of Negro Women (http://www.ncnw.org/resources/index.htm) can direct you to resources for health, advocacy, and financial empowerment.

- For Hispanic women, the National Council of La Raza (http://www.nclr.org) can help with education, entrepreneurship, and community participation opportunities.

Health Care and Advice for You and/or Your Children

- Contact your city or state's department of health and human services, or visit:

- Insure Kids Now! (http://www.insurekidsnow.gov) links to programs in every state that make health insurance coverage available to children under 18.

- One in three Latina women has no health insurance. For help accessing quality health care and advice, visit http://www.4woman.gov/minority/hispanicamerican. You can also call their Information and Referral Service at 1-800-994-9662 or by TDD at 1-888-220-5446. ¡Recursos en Español!

- The U.S. Indian Health Service (http://www.ihs.gov) provides resources on maternal and child health, as well as domestic violence, substance abuse, and mental-health treatment resources for women of Native American /Alaskan Native descent. Visit them on the Internet or call (888) 830-7280.

- Planned Parenthood: http://www.plannedparenthood.org. This organization provides basic women's and reproductive care for a reduced fee, along with safer-sex supplies, counseling, and resources such as books, videos, and DVDs to help you make informed choices about your health.

- The News for Women's Health Outpost (http://www.nwho.org) lets you find information on common women's health topics such as nutrition, pregnancy, depression, breast health, and weight loss. Click a search term on the main page, and you will be taken to a page with many search results on the topic you have chosen.

Ex-offender moms have to establish a new, positive relationship with their children. They may be able to do this through fun, inexpensive outings or art and craft activities. Photo: U.S. Fish and Wildlife Service.

SHE NEVER GAVE UP

Kathy is in her mid-twenties and has five children. She lived in Section 8 housing—until she was evicted on a drug charge. She was placed on probation for three years, and three of her children went to another state to stay with her mother, while she and her two remaining children moved into her aunt's house. After a year, when the family of six had been reunited, Kathy's relationship with her aunt fell apart, and out she went.

Working a series of dead-end jobs and alternating stays in one shelter after another, Kathy obtained a job as a motel housekeeper, and moved up to a supervisory position within six months. She moved her family into the motel. With stable housing and employment, she was able to save enough money to rent an apartment. She has continued to work full time and has applied to beauty school to fulfill her dream of becoming a hairstylist.

Sometimes it is hard to cope with all the pressure, but if you can take a parenting course while inside, then dealing with your children when you are released will be easier.

BOOKS BY WOMEN, FOR WOMEN

Picking Up the Pieces: A Workbook for Incarcerated Women. Beverly Kay Welo's 2004 workbook, designed for your use on the inside, can provide great support once you are released. Stories, pictures, and activities can help you understand grief, loss, and recovery. This book is available for a fee from American Correctional Association at www.aca.org/bookstore or (800) 222-5646 ext. 0129.

Cage Your Rage for Women. Judith Urquhart and Murray C. Cullen's 2003 workbook can help you manage anger, stress, and other emotions that can be destructive. Tools and questions in this workbook can teach you about yourself, show you healthier ways to express your feelings, and improve your chances of success at work or in school. This book is available for a fee from American Correctional Association at www.aca.org/bookstore or (800) 222-5646 ext. 0129.

How to Be a Responsible Mother, by Diane E. Stawar and Terry L. Stawar (2008), prepares you for the challenges of being a mother on the inside while also readying you for the parenting challenges when you return to the community. Learn how to connect with your children, use positive discipline, and think about your own childhood and what it can teach you. This book is available for a fee from American Correctional Association at www.aca.org/bookstore or (800) 222-5646 ext. 0129.

A Piece of Cake: A Memoir. Three Rivers Press. 2006. Cupcake Brown's early years were marked by drugs, violence, and exploitation. She survived to graduate law school with very high honors, and is now a practicing lawyer. Besides her best-selling book, she has a website at http://www.cupcake-brown.com.

Grace After Midnight: A Memoir, by Felicia Pearson and David Ritz. Boston: Hachette Book Group, 2007. Felicia "Snoop" Pearson, a former youthful offender, earned her GED while incarcerated. Pearson is now involved in the arts, runs a drama program for kids, and had a starring role on HBO's *The Wire*.

Life on the Outside: The Prison Odyssey of Elaine Bartlett, by Jennifer Gonnerman. New York: Farrar, Straus, and Giroux, 2004. Gonnerman, a journalist, helps tell the story of Elaine, a mother of four, who spent sixteen years incarcerated for a drug offense. Her story of reentry, with no job, no home, and a fractured family in New York City, shows the problems and rewards of her release in an honest way.

Style Noir: The First How-to Guide to Fashion Written with Black Women in Mind, by Constance White. Darby, Pennsylvania: Diane Publishing Company, 1998. No matter how much money you have to spend on clothing, a polished first impression can make a big difference. If you need a little help working with what you have, the author provides sensible advice on how to dress for work, accessorize the basics, and learn the advantages of dressing professionally along with inspiring stories of African-American designers and celebrities.

You've Only Got Three Seconds: How to Make the Right Impression in Your Business and Social Life, by Camille Lavington with Stephanie Losse. New York: Main Street Books, 1998. Make a great first impression and find your self-confidence. From the best way to keep a neat appearance to the best way to behave in an office setting, self-assessment quizzes help you emphasize your strongest points.

COMPUTERS AND THE INTERNET

THAT WAS THEN–THIS IS NOW

One major change since this book's initial publication is the world's use of computers and the Internet. With the Internet, you have virtually any information at your fingertips. You can conduct your job search through the Internet. Many companies let you apply for jobs online, and companies such as Target, Wal-Mart, Home Depot, and some grocery store chains have kiosks in their stores so you can complete applications online, right at the store.

One-stop career centers and libraries have computers you can use to gain an advantage in your job search. You can hunt for jobs on the Internet even if you do not have a computer at home.

Unfortunately, most prisons and jails do not allow Internet access. There are still a number of things you can do to prepare yourself for employment before your release!

No matter what your age, you can become computer literate.

COMPUTERS 101 AND THE INTERNET

Photo: Wikimedia Commons.

Computers and the Internet have changed our way of life by making information and communication much more easily available. Everything is a keystroke away. Why is this important to you? Practically every business, even a restaurant, uses some form of a computer.

What is the Internet?

It is a huge global network of computers sharing information together.

What is a search engine?

A search engine is an Internet tool for locating information. There are many to choose from. Visit www.google.com, www.yahoo.com, or your internet service provider's home page. Type in employment resources for ex-offenders and the search engine will find hundreds of websites on that topic.

What is a website?

A website is a company's "home" on the Internet. At websites such as www.pepco.com, you can learn about the company or organization, the kind of people who work for them, and often whether they are hiring or what job openings they may have.

Getting a Free E-mail Address

E-mail is electronic mail. You can send a letter, information, photographs, and other media through the Internet via E-mail, and it will arrive anywhere in the world in seconds. Some E-mail accounts, such as those offered at www.gmail.com, www.hotmail.com, and mail.yahoo.com, are free. You can access them from any computer, in a library, a coffee shop, or your home. Just be sure to LOG OUT of your E-mail if you are using it on a computer you share with others.

IF YOU DO NOT HAVE A COMPUTER or DO NOT KNOW HOW TO USE ONE

A 59-year-old parolee had been in and out of prison several times. Upon his recent release, he was in my office. I tried to discuss job searching on the Internet. He blurted out, "I don't know how to use a computer!"

"The library has free computers and classes."

"I've never been to the library!"

Learning how to use a computer is no longer an option. It is a necessity! When you learn to use a computer, the world opens to you. Most libraries have free computer use. Some offer free computer-training classes, too. Many community-based social service centers have computers along with one-stop career centers. You do not have to be a whiz. You just need the basics. Learn how to surf the Internet, send E-mail, and do word processing tasks. You can pick up these skills in one afternoon.

If you do not have Internet access, many cities have cyberspace coffee shops where you can purchase access, or get it for free with the purchase of food or drink. As a last resort (due to its high cost), FedEx Kinko's offers Internet access service at $12.00 an hour.

Computer and Internet use is usually a free privilege for library cardholders. Generally, it's easy to get a library card. Photo: Lauren Valdes for the Electronic Resource, Information Competency, and Web 2.0 Outreach Project.

INTERNET RESOURCES

Dress the Part

www.careergear.org *This organization provides interview clothing to men.*

www.dressforsuccess.org *A similar project helps women find career-ready clothing.*

Job Search Engines

www.goodwill.com *Goodwill actively helps ex-cons find employment.*

www.backdoorjobs.com/adventure.html *Find adventurous jobs here.*

www.youfoundjobs.com   www.indeed.com/job-search-engine

http://www.felons.view-local-jobs.com   www.coolworks.com

www.snagajob.com

Resources For Older Workers

www.experienceworks.com *This website provides information on training, employment, and community services for low-income senior citizens.*

www.seniorserviceamerica.org *This website offers training and employment opportunities for those fifty-five or older.*

Don't despair. You can become computer savvy quickly.

COMMUNITY RESOURCES

THE SECOND CHANCE ACT

In 2007, the Second Chance Act became law. Finally, the government recognized that those released from prison need more than the clothes on their back, a few coins in their pocket, and a "Good luck, hope not to see you back here."

As a result, grant money is available to organizations helping ex-offenders make a successful transition from prison to the streets. Consequently, organizations are now reaching out to help the offender population. For example, upon an ex-offender's release, he or she is connected with a case manager who may be able to fund three months of housing, introduce the ex-offender to felony-friendly employers, and provide a clothing allowance. All programs vary, and may be set up differently, so you need to inquire in your community.

211- FIRST CALL FOR HELP

This is perhaps the best way to access community resources. 211 is a service of the United Way. They maintain a database of resources for shelter, clothing, medical help, employment, and other needs. They are a national, nonprofit organization. Most of their call centers are available 24 hours a day. Just dial 211 and you will be connected. If you are unable to connect by using 211, look in the telephone book under United Way.

A LIBRARIAN: A LIVING, BREATHING, WALKING ENCYCLOPEDIA

When it comes to finding information, whether you are searching for organizations that help ex-offenders, educational programs, the prison population of Thailand, or even the correct spelling of a word, your local librarian may be your best source of information, and librarians will answer questions over the telephone. Also, remember, libraries may have free Internet access.

Photo: Lauren Valdes for the Electronic Resource, Information Competency, and Web 2.0 Outreach Project.

TRANSPORTATION

An ex-offender reported to the office with a smile on his face, keys dangling from his right hand and a helmet in his left.

"Did you forget your license is suspended?"

"I don't need a license. I bought a scooter that is less than 50cc. I don't even have to have insurance."

Depending on where you live, transportation can be a major hurdle. Some cities have a subway system and/or buses. What do you do if you don't have either of these?

Scooters under 50cc do not require a license or insurance. They have a top speed of 40 miles per hour, and get about 90 miles to a gallon of gas.

NOT ALL STATES PERMIT THE USE OF SCOOTERS IF YOU HAVE HAD A DUI.

CONTACT THE DEPARTMENT OF MOTOR VEHICLES *BEFORE* BUYING ONE!

Photo credit: Vespa. Courtesy of Piaggio Group USA.

HOUSING OPTIONS

It is more difficult to secure housing than employment!

A probationer, upon release from jail, rented a mini-storage space and would sneak in before the gates closed at night, sneaking back out again in the morning. There are other sad stories: some have bought sleeping bags and slept in the woods. Others have slept in boxcars or "couch hop" from friend to friend, quickly wearing out their welcome. Housing is more difficult to find than a job. Most ex-offenders released from jail or prison have limited financial resources. Additionally, many landlords are unwilling to rent to ex-offenders, who may have unlawful detainers (evictions) or otherwise poor rental histories.

Finding a stable housing situation may help restore your family life. Photo: U.S. Fish and Wildlife Service.

PRISON WITHOUT BARS

Being released from incarceration is stressful. You need a job, housing, transportation, food, and so forth. One newly released ex-offender had a heart attack the first week he was out. A halfway house may alleviate some of the challenges you are going to face. A halfway house may not be your ideal option, but it could be a good choice. Yes, you will have a case manager, be screened for drugs, and have to follow rules and a curfew. You will also have the opportunity to secure employment and save money for housing.

This author has worked with those who entered a halfway house and those who have not. Those with halfway house experience generally have a smoother transition into the community.

Halfway house still sound like a bad idea?

OXFORD HOUSE

Oxford Houses are homes for recovering addicts. They have more than 1,200 houses throughout the country. This is a self-supporting, non-profit organization that provides housing to men, women, and sometimes women with children. It is a self-run program providing a recovery house for rehabilitating alcoholics and drug addicts. To be accepted into one of their houses, you must go through a review process in which you are interviewed by other tenants. Rent varies from location to location.

Please note: they are serious about recovery. If you are found to have been consuming alcohol or using illicit drugs, you will be required to leave immediately.

You can contact Oxford House's main office http://www.oxfordhouse.org/userfiles/file/ or write or call:

> Oxford House Inc.
> 1010 Wayne Ave., Suite 300
> Silver Spring, MD 20910
> (800) 587-2916

SINGLE ROOMS

Depending on where you live, some homeowners may have converted their garages into living space. Others may rent out a room in their homes for extra cash. The best resource for locating these unique living situations is www.craigslist.org. Similar to the classified section of a newspaper, it is one of the most popular sites on the Internet. You can find job listings, housing resources, and even post your services in different categories. The best part is that the site is free to those answering ads.

SALVATION ARMY

The Salvation Army offers numerous housing programs, from shelters to single-room occupancies. Type Salvation Army and your state into an Internet search engine. Or, to obtain information on programs in your area, write to:

The Salvation Army National Headquarters
PO Box 269
Alexandria, VA 22313

CATHOLIC CHARITIES

Like the Salvation Army, Catholic Charities has an array of housing programs, including housing counseling, limited financial assistance, temporary shelter, or transitional housing. Visit www.catholiccharitiesusa.org, call (703) 549-1390, or write to:

Catholic Charities USA
66 Canal Center Plaza, Suite 600
Alexandria, VA 22314

UNION MISSIONS

Located around the country, a Union Mission has dormitory-style shelter in which you can usually stay for 30 days at a time. Check your local *Yellow Pages* for listings.

Other options may be available through the YMCA or YWCA in your area.

RENTING AN APARTMENT

If you intend to rent an apartment, apply to smaller, independently owned complexes. Like employers, they may be more flexible. If the landlord is hesitant, and you can afford it, offer to put up a two-month security deposit.

If you do rent, keep in mind that, as with a job, you are trying to build a solid history. Be a model tenant. The first and foremost thing is to pay your rent on time—on or before the due date. As one parolee stated, "Even when I was running the street, I always paid my rent." Another parolee says, "My rent comes before food." This ex-offender eventually bought a trailer.

BUYING A TRAILER

Once you are on your feet and more stable, consider buying a trailer home. Relatively inexpensive compared to a house, it offers a good alternative for ex-offenders.

Housing Options

BUYING A HOUSE

With the collapse of the housing market, many houses were foreclosed upon and are now bank-owned. These houses are priced below market value, but you still need to qualify for a mortgage. To do so, you must have a steady income, a down payment, and a good credit score.

HABITAT FOR HUMANITY

Habitat for Humanity is one of the most successful nonprofit organizations in the country. They build homes for low-income families. All the materials for their homes, as well as the labor, are donated. You will have to go through an approval process to be eligible for one of their homes, and once in the home, you will be required to pay a mortgage. www.habitat.org/cd/local/

The organization founded by this author, **9 to 5 Beats Ten to Life**, owns several properties and rents exclusively to ex-offenders. Other nonprofit organizations specialize in renting to offenders.

This is one of the houses owned by 9 to 5 Beats Ten to Life. *Ex-offenders completed the rehabilitation on this house. It is rented to an ex-offender.*

CAREER ASSESSMENT: JOURNEY OF SELF-DISCOVERY

There are several ways to assess your interests, talents, and personality. Here are a few.

✓   The Career Assessment Inventory is a long questionnaire that helps you identify your interests and likes. It takes about forty-five minutes to complete, and is evaluated by a computer. It compares your responses to others who are in careers in which you are interested.

✓   The General Aptitude Battery Test will test twelve different skill areas. This will help you identify your natural talents and skill sets.

✓   Meyers-Briggs Personality Indicator: If you are going to do only one assessment, do this one. It may help you identify which one of the sixteen different personality types you have. Knowing this may help you find a career that fits your personality.

WARNING!

These three assessments are only guides. Do not make a career decision based solely on the results. They are meant to help you gain a better understanding of yourself and provide you with insight you may not have had.

You may be able to take these tests at a state employment office or at a college counseling office. Many websites offer career assessments or career tests. Try typing career assessment into an Internet search engine. Be aware that some websites are trying to sell you their particular training, school or product.

BOOKS

Do What You Are: Discover the Perfect Career for You through the Secrets of Personality Type, Revised and Updated Edition (2009) by Paul Tieger and Barbara Barron-Tieger, helps you find the career that is right for you by using basic personality type, workbook exercises, and step-by-step instructions for fitting your job search to your needs. New York: Little, Brown, and Co.

I Could Do Anything If I Only Knew What It Was: How to Discover What You Really Want and How to Get It, by Barbara Sher. Take a tough approach to discovering your goals and achieving them. New York: The Bantam Dell Publishing Group, 1995. This is also available as an audiobook.

YOUR OWN CAREER ASSESSMENT

An effective way to do a career assessment is to answer questions, such as the following:

1. What activities have I done for enjoyment?

    _____

2. What activities do I participate in when I lose track of time?

    _____

3. What would I do if I had a complete day for myself? (Be realistic.)

    _____

4. Do I need close supervision, or am I self-directed?

    _____

5. Do I prefer working in a fast-paced environment?

    _____

6. Do I prefer working alone or with others?

    _____

7. What type of books, magazines, movies, or television shows do I enjoy?

    _____

THREE BIG QUESTIONS

1. If I had the education, training, and qualifications necessary, what career or profession would I enter?

    _____

2. If I were financially secure (but wanted to work), what type of work would I do?

    _____

3. If I knew I could not fail at a job or career, what would it be?

    _____

DON'T STOP NOW—RESEARCH!

Based on the previous pages, make a list of careers you might like. Now, it is time to research your careers.

In what careers are you interested?

_____   _____
_____   _____
_____   _____

You want to know:

1. How much demand is there for that field?

   _____
   _____

2. How many job openings are projected in the next several years?

   _____
   _____

3. What type of training is needed, and how long will it take?

   _____
   _____

4. What is the starting salary? The long-term potential salary?

   _____
   _____

*You can find all this information through the **Occupational Outlook Handbook**, available in your library and in some career centers. Parts of it are also available online.*

YOUR EDUCATION:
ONE MORE STEP ON THE JOURNEY OF SELF-DISCOVERY

1. If you could learn about any one thing, what would it be?

    _____

2. Do you see yourself continuing your education past your high school or technical diploma? Past college? If not, why not?

    _____

    _____

3. What did you want to be "when I grow up?" Is it still true? What educational path could you take to get there?

    _____

    _____

Answer these questions, and refer to the career self-discovery questions you answered on page 94. Then, contact an admissions counselor at one of the institutions you listed on page 105 to see if one of its programs meets your needs.

THE *YELLOW PAGES* ASSESSMENT

Go through the index of any telephone directory from A to Z, and make a list of anything in which you are interested. You may see a pattern, or spark a new area of interest.

_____

_____

_____

_____

_____

_____

_____

Remember your passions, talents, and interests are all keys to your future success.

BOOK

The Big Book of Jobs 2009-2010, by McGraw Hill Editors. It is the size of a telephone book, and lists hundreds of job titles including the job outlook, the nature of the work, training, qualifications required, and earnings. You can order it from http://mhprofessional.com/product.php?isbn=0071602046 .

MORE HEART ATTACKS OCCUR ON MONDAY THAN ANY OTHER DAY

Is it the stress of going to a job they do not like?

It is early Monday morning, and I am standing on the subway in Washington, DC. As I glance down the aisle, I do not see a smile on anyone's face. Are they tired or hung over? Or, is it that they do not look forward to going to work, and would rather be doing something else?

Each week has 168 hours and adults spend the greatest number of hours of their lives at work. So, why would anyone work at a job that they do not enjoy? Some need to, for survival, but we all have opportunities to pursue jobs of our choice. It takes sacrifice and daily dedication.

For example, two women work in the same office in clerical positions. One pursues her education at night and earns a degree. After receiving her degree, she is promoted to a position of greater responsibility, which brings an increase in pay. The other person does not advance and in a company downsizing, she is laid off.

Discover the field you most want to pursue, research what it takes to gain qualifications, and begin the process.

I am keenly aware that you may be reading this while incarcerated, and thinking about a career is unrealistic from your vantage point. No argument here—it is. Once you are stable in the community, have a steady job, and housing, you can pursue other opportunities. At this point, look ahead two or three years—where do you want to be and what do you want to be doing? Those two or three years are going to pass regardless of what you decide.

The choice is yours.

LEARN MORE: EARN MORE

Education or training may be an opportunity to meet other people—to gain new friends. Photo: Wikimedia Commons.

NO HIGH SCHOOL DIPLOMA OR GED?

GET YOUR GED OR DIPLOMA

When entering prison, he was reading at the third-grade level. While incarcerated, he studied toward his GED but sadly did not complete it. Upon his release, he enrolled at an adult education program and passed the test. When he reported to his probation officer, he commented: "I feel that I conquered the world." Certainly, this accomplishment boosted his self-esteem! And, it could do the same for you.

To enroll in an apprenticeship program, you will need a high school diploma or a GED. If you do not have one, you have options with which to earn it.

Here are some of the many options available to you. You can do the following:

- Enroll in an adult learning class

- Take an online class, particularly if you are computer savvy

- Do self-study through GED books available at your local library. Prior to placement in a GED program, you may score high enough to test out, meaning you will have no need for formal classes, but you will go directly to take the GED test.

Use this space to list your local resources for programs that can help you obtain your GED, earn your high school diploma, or improve your basic skills through adult education programs. In the telephone book, look under community center or learning center to begin.

_____

_____

_____

_____

_____

_____

_____

_____

LEARNING ON THE JOB

You can still make it! Many people did not graduate from high school but are doing well in their field. They learned on the job and took courses that helped them to improve their skills or develop new ones. A few examples include:

- Auto mechanic
- Auto painter/repairer
- Bricklayer
- Carpenter
- Cook/chef
- Drywall installer
- Floor covering installer
- Floral designer
- Meat cutter
- Ironworker

TOP TEN JOBS – NO EDUCATION REQUIRED

1. Retail salesperson
2. Customer service representative
3. Food service worker
4. Office clerk
5. Janitor/cleaner
6. Waiter/waitress
7. Road kill collector
8. Portable toilet cleaner
9. Crime scene cleaner
10. Migrant field worker

These jobs pay less than $10.00 an hour, and most pay barely above the minimum wage.

Learn More: Earn More

LACK OF EDUCATION

Many of you reading this may have dropped out of high school or may lack formal education or skills to offer an employer. Why did you leave school? Perhaps you were bored, or the subjects did not interest you. You now cringe at the thought of returning to school. Going to school to learn about a specific field or trade that interests you, however, can make a huge difference.

For example, would you like to be an automotive technician, a cosmetologist, or a veterinary technician? If so, enroll in a school that specializes in your selected area of study, and any class you take will have a direct correlation to your chosen job.

Reading to your children gives them an advantage when they start school. It may help them avoid following in your footsteps to prison.

"I was tired of earning minimum wage, so I returned to school."

DETERMINATION

Diane works nights and weekends at an upscale restaurant as a cook. This was a paycheck, not a career. She enrolled in a vocational program for dental assistants and has recently completed her first semester.

NEVER SAID IT WOULD BE EASY

Distraught, Leon reported to the office. He had been working dead-end jobs for over a year, and commented, "You cannot make it out here without a trade." So, he enrolled in auto tech training.

Fast forward: you have returned to the community, settled in with a job, and have stable housing. However, you are not thrilled with the kind of work you are doing, which gives little or no opportunity for advancement.

This is where a secondary education comes into play. I am aware that many of you reading this book have had poor experiences in school. Most likely, you were just bored with the classes. I am not suggesting you return to a traditional school; rather, find a specialized training course to prepare you for a job you would enjoy. For instance, do you like working on motorcycles? You could attend a Harley Davidson Training School and work on the "King of Cycles."

Educational training programs are endlessly varied, giving you boundless opportunities. Once you are studying in a field of your choice, you may find that learning is enjoyable, and you will look forward to each day, embracing rather than dreading school. By taking an active role in choosing a field in which you will excel, you can find a program that gives you a strong connection to your future dream career.

103

GET INSPIRED: VOCATIONAL/TRADE SCHOOL

After being in and out of prison four times, a forty-year-old man enrolled in a vocational school for auto technicians and completed an eighteen-month program. He now earns $1,500 a week, which is $78,000 annually.

Diving for Hope

A program in a California correctional facility has a vocational training program that teaches underwater welding to inmates. Underwater welding is one of the few high-paying, in-demand jobs available for a hard worker without a college or even a high school diploma. It takes intense training, but the rewards are great. "I make more money diving than I ever did as a safecracker."

No, you're not going to transfer to this prison. This illustrates that you do not have to continue to work for low wages in jobs you do not enjoy. With some training or education, you could also work as an underwater welder, or in numerous other careers that catch your interest.

> "Develop skills in an area of your interest so that when you complete training, you are working in a field of your choice."
> **Carl Z., Parolee**
>
> "I love school. Why? It's taking me somewhere in my life."
> **Steve W., Former Inmate**
>
> "Without a trade. Jobs don't pay enough." Tired of working at jobs without a future, he is studying computer technology.
> **William G., Ex-Offender**

STUDY SUBJECTS THAT INTEREST YOU

When you study subjects in which you are interested, it is not like going to school. Your area has many schools and training programs. Start from the telephone directory or the Internet, and list them here.

I'm Interested in

_____

_____

_____

Vocational Schools and Programs:

Program: _____

School: _____

Address: _____

City/State/ZIP: _____

Telephone: _____

E-mail: _____

Website: _____

Program: _____

School: _____

Address: _____

City/State/ZIP: _____

Telephone: _____

E-mail: _____

Website: _____

Community Colleges:

Name of school: _____

Name of program: _____

Address: _____

City/State/ZIP: _____

Telephone: _____

E-mail: _____

Name of school: _____

Name of program: _____

Address: _____

City/State/ZIP: _____

Telephone: _____

E-mail: _____

Name of school: _____

Name of program: _____

Address: _____

City/State/ZIP: _____

Telephone: _____

E-mail: _____

Name of school: _____

Name of program: _____

Address: _____

City/State/ZIP: _____

Telephone: _____

E-mail: _____

Learn More: Earn More

APPRENTICESHIP PROGRAMS

In lieu of being sentenced to incarceration, the court ordered a probationer to enter and complete an apprenticeship program. She chose an electrician program. She is currently in the third year of her apprenticeship, earning $17.00 an hour. Once she receives her license, she will earn $40,000 a year.

An apprenticeship program combines working a job under a journeyperson's direction with classroom work. You will learn a trade on the job, while earning a paycheck. Most apprenticeships take an average of three years on the job, plus 144 hours of classroom work. For more information, write to:

Office of Apprenticeship
Francis Perkins Building
200 Constitution Ave., NW
Washington, DC 20210
(877) US-2JOBS

Visit http://www.doleta.gov/oa and explore a variety of apprenticeship options.

Your local resources:

_____
_____
_____
_____
_____
_____
_____
_____
_____
_____
_____
_____

IS A COLLEGE DEGREE REQUIRED?

On the first day of his freshman year in college, an ex-offender attended a philosophy class. As he was listening to the college professor, he thought, how is this going to help me make a living? That was his first and last day of college. Don't misunderstand; in some professions, you absolutely need a degree. However, you do not necessarily need a degree. College may be overrated. Currently, there are more college graduates annually than there are jobs.

With that said, you do need *some form of training*, whether it is through an apprenticeship program, a trade school, a certificate program, or other means. There are numerous ways to learn.

SELF-DIRECTED LEARNING

"I can learn anything I need or want to. The library has all the information I need."

One ex-offender was a handyman. He always had this book, as large as the *Yellow Pages*, with him—a book about home improvement and repairs. As long as he has had this book, rarely has there been a time he could not make a needed repair.

Not only does the library have information about any subject you can think of, information is also available online. If that is not enough, you can spend the entire day at a bookstore, finding books on anything and everything you want.

LEARN AS YOU GO

CDs and DVDs are available on almost any subject, many of which you can listen to while driving. DVDs from the library are usually free.

BOOKS

The *Cool Careers Without College* series (Princeton: Peterson's Guides), by a variety of authors, covers a huge range of interests, from computers and health care to fitness, nature, fashion, and travel.

WAYS TO IMPROVE YOUR KNOWLEDGE and EDUCATION

- ❑ 4 years of college
- ❑ 2 years of community college (associate's degree)
- ❑ Vocational/trade school
- ❑ Apprenticeship program
- ❑ Online classes
- ❑ Short-term certificate training
- ❑ Self-directed learning
- ❑ One-day seminars
- ❑ On-the-job training
- ❑ DVDs

Education is one of the keys to a stable future. Consider what type of training will get you where you want to be. Photo: Sekhar Lukose Kuriakose.

IS A DEGREE IN YOUR FUTURE?

What education is needed for your dream job? A college degree may be useful for you.

PROOF POSITIVE

While on probation Juanita completed her social work degree. Upon her release from probation, she graduated from college, continuing directly to graduate school to earn her master's degree. Now, she works in a social service organization, providing assistance to ex-offenders and those on welfare. She owns a house and a very nice car—proof of her accomplishments.

Many ex-offenders have gone on to work in counseling positions and as chemical dependency counselors to help others change their lives.

With a high school diploma, more doors are open for you. Even more are open for those with a college degree. Photo: Wikimedia Commons.

109

FINANCIAL AID FOR EDUCATION

Federal student financial aid consists of Stafford loans, PLUS loans, consolidation loans, Federal Supplemental Educational Opportunity Grants (FSEOGs), federal work-study, Perkins loans, and Pell grants. A Pell grant, unlike a loan, does not have to be repaid. Generally, Pell grants are awarded only to undergraduate students who have not earned a bachelor's or professional degree. Unfortunately, they are not available while you are incarcerated. For more information on federal student financial aid, or to obtain a Free Application for Federal Student Aid (FAFSA), call or write:

(800) 4-FED-AID (433-3243)

Federal Student Aid Information Center
PO Box 84
Washington, DC 20004

A word to the wise: if you take out a loan and do not finish your education, you are still responsible for repaying the loan. The government is relentless in wanting this loan paid back.

DEFAULT ON FEDERAL STUDENT LOANS

How can you regain eligibility for federal and state financial aid if you are returning to school after defaulting on a student loan? If you make six reasonable monthly payments in a row, you can bring your loan out of default. That does not free you from your obligation to repay, but it may restore your eligibility for assistance.

Financial aid eligibility will be reinstated to defaulted borrowers who enter into a repayment arrangement and make a minimum of six consecutive on-time payments. You must make a telephone or written request for reinstatement, and you must continue to make these monthly payments to retain future eligibility. Reinstatement is a one-time opportunity, and the process cannot be restarted once begun.

Write to the Student Assistance Commission in your state of residence, or search for Student Assistance Commission on the Internet to get the process started. If it is going to take some effort to track down your student loan records, start by contacting:

U.S. Department of Education
Debt Collection Service
600 Independence Ave., SW
Washington, DC 20202

You may also call (800) 621-3115.

SCHOLARSHIPS CAN HELP WITH COSTS

Talbot's Women's Scholarship Fund

If you are a woman and earned a high school diploma or GED prior to September 1992, are enrolled or are planning to enroll in a full or part-time undergraduate course of study at a two- or four-year college, and have at least two semesters remaining to complete your first undergraduate degree, visit www.talbots.com/about/scholar/scholar.asp.

USA Funds "Access to Education" Scholarship

USA Funds will award renewable $1,500 scholarships to full-time graduate students with financial need. You must be enrolled for the entire academic year, from fall to spring. Applicants must also have an annual income of $35,000 or less, be U.S. citizens or eligible non-citizens; and must not currently be in default on any student loans. Applications and additional information are available on the USA Funds website at www.usafunds.org or by faxing an application request with your name and mailing address to (888) 546-4107.

Other Scholarships and Loan Programs

Your local library has information on other scholarships and loan programs for which you may be eligible. A bit of research can reward you with big dollars toward your education.

BOOKS TO PRISONERS

"I believe that education through books is the only vehicle to change whether in or out of prison. I would be lost without books and the folks who sent them."

The majority of prisons and jails do not allow inmates to receive books from family or friends. They must come directly from a bookstore, the publisher, or a service such as Amazon.com. However, several bookstores have set up non-profit organizations to send books free of charge to inmates. The following organizations send books to prisoners—some places have geographic or other restrictions. Read through the list and see if there is a service in your area. You may request books by subject or topic. The individuals shipping these books to you are donating their time, so be patient.

APPALACHIAN PRISON BOOK PROJECT (APBP)
PO Box 601
Morgantown, WV 26501
appalachianpbp@gmail.com
Free books to prisoners in KY, OH, MD, VA, WV.

ASHEVILLE PRISON BOOKS
c/o Downtown Books and News
67 N. Lexington Ave.
Asheville, NC 28801
E-mail twothirds@riseup.net

BELLINGHAM BOOKS TO PRISONERS
PO Box 1254
Bellingham, WA 98227
(360) 733-9099

BOOK 'EM
PO Box 71357
Pittsburgh, PA 15213
bookem@keromail.com
www.prisoners.com/bookemi.html
Free books to prisoners in all states except OR and in TX to women only.

BOOKS THROUGH BARS
4722 Baltimore Ave.
Philadelphia, PA 19143
(215) 727-8170
www.booksthroughbars.org
Sends progressive political and educational materials at no charge to county, state, and federal prisoners in the Mid Atlantic region (DE, MD, NJ, NY, PA, VA, WV). Also sends to jails and halfway houses in this area.

BOOKS THROUGH BARS - NYC
c/o Bluestockings Bookstore
172 Allen St.
New York, NY 10002
(212) 254-3697, ext. 326
www.abcnorio.org/affiliated/btb.html
Ships to prisoners nationwide.

BOOKS THRU BARS OF ITHACA
Second Floor
c/o Autumn Leaves Bookstore
115 The Commons
Ithaca, NY 14850
Sends books free of charge to prisoners in CT, DE, ME, MA, MD, NH, NJ, NY, PA, RI, VT.

BOOKS TO OREGON PRISONERS
PO BOX 11222
Portland, OR 97211
http://www.bookstooregonprisoners.org
Free books to OR prisoners only.

BOOKS TO PRISONERS
c/o Left Bank Books
92 Pike St., Box A
Seattle, WA 98101
www.bookstoprisoners.net
Free books to prisoners to all states except CA. Does not ship to prisons that require all books be sent new.

CHICAGO BOOKS TO WOMEN IN PRISON
c/o Beyond Media Education
4001 N. Ravenswood Ave.
Chicago, IL 60613
http://www.chicagobwp.org
E chicagobw@hotmail.com
Free books to women prisoners in CT, FL, IL, IN, MS, OH.

CLEVELAND BOOKS 2 PRISONERS
PO Box 602440
Cleveland, OH 44102
Clevelandbooks2prisoners@hotmail.com
Free books for prisoners in OH only.

D.C. BOOKS TO PRISONS
PO Box 5243
Hyattsville, MD 20782
http://www.quixote.org/ej/bookstoprisons
bookstoprisons@mutualaid.org
Prison restrictions and subjects and authors of interest. No catalogs. We try to send everywhere but may NOT send to the following when swamped: IL, MA, NH, NJ, NY, PA, OR, or WA.

GAINESVILLE BOOKS FOR PRISONERS
PO Box 12164
Gainesville, FL 32604
http://www.civicmediacenter.org/links/2003/11/01/13.29.05.htm

INSIDE BOOKS PROJECT
c/o 12th St. Books
827 W 12th St
Austin, TX 78701
www.insidebooksproject.org
Sends free books and literature to prisoners in TX only. Send one 41 cent stamp for TX – prisoner-focused newsletter. Accepts artwork donations for their yearly prisoner art show.

INTERNATIONALIST PRISON BOOKS COLLECTIVE
405 W. Franklin St.
Chapel Hill, NC 27516
www.prisonbooks.info
New program that sends books to AL, MS, and LA.

LOUISIANA BOOKS 2 PRISONERS
831 Elysian Fields #143
New Orleans, LA 70117
books2prisoners@riseup.net

MIDWEST BOOKS TO PRISONERS
c/o Quimby's Bookstore
1321 N. Milwaukee Ave. PMB #460
Chicago, IL 60622
www.freewebs.com/mwbtp
Serves IA, IL, KS, MO, MN, NE, WI.

MIDWEST PAGES TO PRISONERS PROJECT
c/o Boxcar Books
408 E. 6th St.
Bloomington, IN 47408-4018
(812) 339-8710
http://www.pagestoprisoners.org/
Priority is given to requests from women's and youth facilities.

OLYMPIA BOOKS TO PRISONERS
PO Box 912
Olympia, WA 98507
Voicemail: (360) 352-5460

PORTLAND BOOKS TO PRISONERS
PO Box 1222
1112 NE Morton
Portland, OR 97211
*If you are incarcerated in a facility that
does not allow used books, Portland Books
to Prisoners has a selection of new books that
meet most institutions' criteria.*

PRISON BOOK PROGRAM
c/o United First Parish Church
1306 Hancock St., Ste 100
Quincy, MA 02169
info@prisonbookprogram.org
http://www.prisonbookprogram.org/
Covers prisoners in all states except
CA, MD, MI, NV, and TX.
Does not offer true crime or white suprema-
cist books. Publishes the *National Prisoner
Resource List*— free to prisoners nationwide
upon request.

PRISON BOOK PROJECT
c/o Food for Thought Books
PO Box 396
Amherst, MA 01004-0396
(413) 584-8975 ext. 208
www.prisonbooks.org
Serves prisoners in New England states
(CT, NH, ME, MA, RI, VT) and TX only.
Request books by topics of interest, not title.
No mailing list or catalog. No hardback books.

THE PRISON LIBRARY PROJECT
PMB 128
915-C W. Foothill Blvd.
Claremont, CA 91711-3356
http://www.claremontforum.org/
Free books on self-help, personal and spiritual
growth, wellness, and metaphysical books.
No law books, technical, or GED. No catalog.
Free resource guide on request.

PRISON LITERATURE PROJECT
c/o Bound Together Bookstore
1369 Haight St.
San Francisco, CA 94117
(415) 672-7858
prisonlit@yahoo.com
No TX requests. Request types of books–not
specific titles.

READ BETWEEN THE BARS
c/o Daily Planet Publishing
PO Box 1589
Tucson, AZ 85702
http://www.readbetweenthebars.org/
readbetweenthebars@gmail.com
Sends books to prisoners in AZ.

THE READERS CORNER
Prison Book Program
31 Montford Ave.
Asheville, NC 28801
prisonbooks31@hotmail.com
http://www.main.nc.us/prisonbooks/
Sends free books to prisoners in GA, NC, SC,
and TN only.

SEATTLE BOOKS TO PRISONERS
c/o Left Bank Books
92 Pike St., Box A
Seattle, WA 98101
(206) 442-2013
bookstoprisoners@cs.com
www.bookstoprisoners.net

**URBANA - CHAMPAIGN BOOKS TO
PRISONERS PROJECT**
c/o Spineless Books
PO Box 515
Urbana, IL 61803
www.books2prisoners.org
ucbtp@yahoogroups.com (listserve)
Sends all types of books to state and federal
prisoners in IL. Has a large selection of novels
and popular genres such as African-American
history and literature, and dictionaries.

**WISCONSIN BOOKS TO PRISONERS/
RAINBOW BOOKS**
426 W. Gilman St.
Madison, WI 53703
(608) 262-9036
www.rainbowbookstore.org/b2p

WOMENS PRISON BOOK PROJECT
c/o Arise Bookstore
2441 Lyndale Ave. S.
Minneapolis, MN 55405
(612) 721-3723
womensprisonbookproject@gmail.com
http://www.wpbp.org
Ships to all states except CO, MI, OR, WV.
Free books to women prisoners only. No
county jail requests. No hardback books.

Books for Inspiration and Self-Help for Men and Women

Cooked: From the Streets to the Stove, From Cocaine to Foie Gras, by Jeff Henderson. "Chef Jeff" served time for drug-related offenses. Now he owns a successful catering company, Posh Urban Cuisine, and was featured on the Food Network's *Chef Jeff Project*. New York: William Morrow, 2007.

Manchild in the Promised Land, by Claude Brown. This individual overcame his criminal past and made a success of his life. New York: Signet, 1965.

Makes Me Wanna Holler, by Nathan McCall. McCall was a journalist for the *Washington Post*. This book tells the story of a violent youth and his subsequent imprisonment and release. New York: Random House, 1994.

Coming Out of the Ice: An Unexpected Life, by Victor Herman. This 1967 book, about a young man imprisoned in Soviet labor camps, is out of print, but you may be able to find it at your local library. An audio CD version (2002) is also available.

The Kid: A True Story, by Kevin Lewis. Abused by his parents, mistreated by authorities, and exposed to a life of crime as a teenager, Lewis eventually succeeded in taking control of his life. New York: Penguin Books, 2004.

Life After Loss, by Beverly Welo. Learn how to resolve feelings in a positive manner and stop the cycle of negative choices that led to your incarceration. Issues discussed include death and loss, the cycle of grief, pain avoidance and substance abuse, grief and incarceration, denial and protest, acceptance, and resolution. This book is available for a fee from American Correctional Association at www.aca.org/bookstore or (800) 222-5646 ext. 0129.

99 Ways to Stay Unemployed, by Mike Davis

OTHER MATERIALS

The video *9 to 5 Beats Ten to Life* is available for a fee from the American Correctional Association at www.aca.org/bookstore or (800) 222-5646 ext. 0129.

Contact the author, Mike Davis, at fromcontocareer@yahoo.com for other material his organization has produced.

Your Master Plan

After going through this book, lay out the steps you are going to take when you are released:

1. Where are you going to apply for jobs?
   _____
   _____

2. How are you going to get to and from your job?
   _____
   _____
   _____

3. Where are you going to live? Why?
   _____
   _____

4. What community resources are you going to use and what do you expect they will do for you?
   _____
   _____
   _____

5. Where are you going to get clothing for your job interviews and your job?
   _____
   _____

6. What telephone number are you going to use on your resume?
   _____

7. What E-mail address are you going to use on your resume?
   _____

8. Where are you going to go if you have a medical problem?
   _____

9. Where are you going to go to get necessary prescription drugs?
   _____

10. Where are you going to go if you have a dental problem?
    _____

11. Where can you get mental health counseling?
    _____

12. Where will you attend 12-Step meetings?
    _____

APPENDIX A

HOW TO GET VITAL RECORDS

Send a request with the following information to the proper state listed below:

Mother's maiden name
Father's name
Your relationship to the person who needs the record
The purpose for which you need the record
Requestor's name and address
Requestor's driver's license number and state (some states require a photocopy of your ID) if you have this.

If you are incarcerated and cannot find the addresses and information you need to obtain vital records, you may call the state contact numbers listed below. Ask your counselor or case manager for assistance. You should include a letter from your case manager or counselor indicating that you are who you claim to be for the purpose of obtaining the record you need.

Fees for vital records services are subject to change.

Note: www.vitalchek.com now processes requests for birth certificates from all 50 states and Puerto Rico online. There are substantial fees for this service, but you can receive your documentation in as few as three days. States have no contractual relationship with VitalChek and do not warrant or endorse the privacy policy of VitalChek Network, Inc.

Alabama
PO Box 5625
Montgomery, AL 36103-5625
(334) 206-5418
Fax: (334) 262-9563
Birth certificate: $12.00

Alaska
Bureau of Vital Statistics
5441 Commercial Blvd.
PO Box 110675
Juneau, AK 99801
(907) 465-3391
Birth certificate: $20.00

American Samoa
Office of Vital Statistics
Department of Homeland Security
American Samoa Government
PO Box 6894
Pago Pago, American Samoa 96799
(684) 633-1405
Fax (684) 633-6414
Birth certificate: $10.00

Arizona
1818 West Adams
PO Box 3887
Phoenix, AZ 85030-3887
(602) 364-1300
Fax: (602) 249-3040
Birth certificate: $10.00

119

Arkansas
Department of Health
Division of Vital Records, Slot 44
4815 Markham St.
Little Rock, AR 72205
(800) 637-9314
Fax: (501) 663-2832

Colorado
Vital Records Section
4300 Cherry Creek Dr. S.
HS VRD-VA-A-1
Denver, CO 80246-1530
Phone: (303) 692-2200
Birth certificate: $17.75

Connecticut
State of Connecticut Department of Public
Health
Vital Records Section, Customer Services
410 Capitol Ave., MS# 11VRS
PO Box 340308
Hartford, CT 06134-0308
(860) 509-7897
Call for cost information.

Delaware
Office of Vital Statistics
Jesse S. Cooper Bldg.
417 Federal St.
Dover, DE 19901
(302) 744-4549
Fax (302) 736-1862
Birth Certificate: $8.00

District of Columbia
District of Columbia Vital Records Office
825 N. Capital St., NE
Washington, DC 20002
(202) 442-9009
Fax (202) 783-0136
Birth Certificate: $12.00 (short form)/$18.00
(long form)

Florida
Office of Vital Statistics
Attn: Customer Services
PO Box 210
Jacksonville, FL 32231-0042
(904) 359-6900
Costs vary – call for information.

Georgia
Vital Records
2600 Skyland Dr., NE
Atlanta, GA 30319-3640
(404) 679-4702
Fax (404) 524-4278
E-mail: phvitalrecords@gdph.state.ga.us
Birth Certificate: $10.00

Guam
Office of Vital Statistics
Department of Public Health and Social Services
PO Box 2816
Agana, GU 96932
(671) 735-7263
Birth Certificate: $5.00

Hawaii
State Department of Health
Office of Health Status Monitoring
Issuance/Vital Statistics Section
PO Box 3378
Honolulu, HI 96801
(808) 586-4539 or (808) 586-4542
Birth Certificate: $10.00

Idaho
Bureau of Vital Records and Health Statistics
450 W. State St.
Boise, ID 83702
(208) 334-5988
Birth Certificate: $13.00

Illinois

Division of Vital Records
Illinois Department of Public Health
605 W. Jefferson St.
Springfield, IL 67202-5097
(217) 782-6553
Birth Certificate: $10.00

Indiana

Vital Records Department
Indiana State Department of Health
PO Box 7125
Indianapolis, IN 46206
(317) 233-2700
Fax (317) 233-7210
Birth Certificate: $10.00

Iowa

Vital Records Section
Lucas State Office Building
321 E. 12th St.
Des Moines, IA 50319-0075
(515) 281-4944
Birth Certificate: $10.00

Kansas

Office of Vital Statistics
1000 S. W. Jackson, Suite 120
Topeka, KS 66612
(785) 296-3253
Fax (785) 357-4332
E-mail: info@kdhe.state.ks.us
Birth Certificate: $12.00

Kentucky

Office of Vital Statistics
275 E. Main St. 1E-A
Frankfort, KY 40621
(502) 564-4212
Fax (502) 227-0032
Birth Certificate: $10.00

Louisiana

Office of Public Health
Vital Records Registry
PO Box 60630
New Orleans, LA 70160
(504) 568-5152 or (800) 454-9570
E-mail: vitalweb@dhh.state.la.us
Birth Certificate: $15.00

Maine

Vital Records
11 State House Station
244 Water St.
Augusta, ME 04333-0011
(207) 287-3181
Birth Certificate: $15.00

Maryland

The Division of Vital Records
6550 Reisterstown Rd.
Reisterstown Road Plaza
Baltimore, MD 21215
(410) 764-3038
Birth Certificate: $12.00

Massachusetts

150 Mount Vernon St., 1st Fl.
Dorchester, MA 02125-3105
(617) 740-2600
Birth Certificate: $19.50 first certified copy;
each additional copy of same record is $14.00

Michigan

Vital Records Requests
PO Box 30721
Lansing, MI 48909
(517) 335-8666
Birth Certificate: $26.00 ($7.00 for
senior citizens)

Minnesota
Minnesota Department of Health
Attention: Office of the State Registrar/ Birth
Certificates
PO Box 64499
St. Paul, MN 55164-0499
(612) 676-5120
Birth Certificate: $16.00

Mississippi
Mississippi Vital Records
PO Box 1700
Jackson, MS 39215-1700
(601) 576-7981
Birth Certificate: $15.00

Missouri
Bureau of Vital Records
PO Box 570
Jefferson City, MO 65102-0570
(573) 751-6400
Birth Certificate: $15.00

Montana
Montana Vital Statistics
PO Box 4210
111 N Sanders, Rm 209
Helena, MT 59604-4210
(406) 444-2685
Fax (406) 444-1803
Birth Certificate: $12.00

Nebraska
Nebraska Department of Health and
Human Services
Division of Public Health
Vital Records
PO Box 95065
Lincoln, NE 68509-5065
(402) 471-2871
Birth Certificate: $12.00

Nevada
Office of Vital Records
4150 Technology Way, Suite 104
Carson City, NV 89706
(775) 684-4242
Fax: 775-684-4156
Birth Certificate: $13.00

New Hampshire
Bureau of Vital Records
Health and Welfare Building
6 Hazen Dr.
Concord, NH 03301
(603) 271-4654
Birth Certificate: $12.00

New Jersey
New Jersey Department of Health and Senior
Services
Vital Statistics and Registration
PO Box 370
Trenton, NJ 08625-0370
(609) 292-4087
Costs vary. Call to verify.

New Mexico
New Mexico Vital Records and Health Statistics
Mailing Address: PO Box 26110, Santa Fe, NM
87502
Street Address: 1105 St. Francis Dr.,
Santa Fe, NM 87502
(505) 827-0121
(505) 827-0963 24-Hour Information Line
(877) 284-0963 Credit Card Orders
Fax (505) 984-1048

New York State
Certification Unit
Vital Records Section
PO Box 2602
Albany, NY 12220-2602
(518) 474-3075
Birth Certificate: $15.00

New York City
Division of Vital Records
NYC Department of Health and
Mental Hygiene
125 Worth St, CN4, Rm. 133
New York, NY 10013
(212) 788-4520
Birth Certificate: $15.00

North Carolina
Vital Records
1903 Mail Service Center
Raleigh, NC 27699-1903
(919) 733-3526
Costs vary; call for details.

North Dakota
Division of Vital Records
State Capitol
600 E. Boulevard Ave.
Dept. 301
Bismark, ND 58505-0200
(701) 328-2360
Birth Certificate: $7.00

Ohio
Vital Statistics
246 N. High Street, 1st Fl
Columbus, OH 43216
(614) 466-2531
Birth Certificate: $10.00

Oklahoma
Vital Records Service
Oklahoma State Dept. of Health
1000 NE Tenth, Rm 117
Oklahoma City, OK 73117
(405) 271-4040
Birth Certificate: $5.00

Oregon
PO Box 14050
Portland, OR 97293-0050
(503) 731-4095
Birth Certificate: $15.00

Pennsylvania
Vital Records, State Dept of Health
PO Box 1528
101 S. Mercer St.
New Castle, PA 16103
(724) 656-3100
Fax (724) 652-8951
Birth Certificate: $4.00 (add an extra
$7.00 if faxed)

Puerto Rico
Department of Health
Demographic Registry
PO Box 11854
Fernandez Juncos Station
San Juan, PR 00910
(787) 728-7980
Birth Certificate: $5.00

Rhode Island
Office of Vital Records
Rhode Island Department of Health
3 Capitol Hill, Rm 101
Providence, RI 02908-5097
(401) 222-2811
Birth Certificate: $ 15.00

South Carolina
Division of Vital Records S.C.
DHEC
2600 Bull St.
Columbia, SC 29201
(803) 898-3630
Fax (803) 898-3761
Call for costs.

South Dakota
Vital Records
SD Department of Health
600 E. Capitol
Pierre, SD 57501-2536
(605) 773-4961
Birth Certificate: $10.00

Tennessee
Central Services Building
1st Floor
421 5th Ave. North
Nashville, TN 37247
Phone (615)741-1763
FAX (615)741-9860
Birth Certificate: $ 12.00

Texas
Bureau of Vital Statistics,
Dept. of Health
PO Box 12040
Austin, TX 78711-2040
(512) 458-7111
Fax (512) 458-7711
E-mail: register@tdh.state.tx.us
Birth Certificate: $11.00

Utah
Office of Vital Records and Health Statistics
Utah Department of Health
PO Box 141012
Salt Lake City, UT 84114-1012
(801) 538-6105
Birth Certificate: $12.00

Vermont State Vital Records Office
Vermont Department of Health
Vital Records Section
Mailing Address: PO Box 70,
Burlington, VT 05402
Street Address:108 Cherry St.
Burlington, VT 05402
(802) 863-7275
Birth Certificate: $7.00

Virginia
Office of Vital Records
PO Box 1000
Richmond, VA 23218-1000
(804) 662-6200
Birth Certificate: $10.00

Virgin Islands Saint Croix
Dept. of Health, Vital Statistics
Charles Harwood Memorial Complex
Christiansted, St. Croix, VI 00820
(340) 773-4050
Birth Certificate: $ 15.00

Virgin Islands Saint Thomas
Vital Statistics
Old Municipal Hospital
St. Thomas, VI 00802
(340) 774-1734
Birth Certificate: $15.00

Washington
Department of Health Center for
Health Statistics
PO Box 9709
Olympia WA 98507-9709.
(360) 236-4300
Birth Certificate: $13.00

West Virginia
Vital Registration, Division of Health
350 Capitol St, Rm 165
Charleston, WV 25301-3701
(304) 558-2931
Info: (304) 558-2931
Fax (304) 558-1051
Birth Certificate: $5.00

Wisconsin
Vital Records Office
PO Box 309
Madison, WI 53701-0309
Automated: (608) 266-1371
Service Counter: (608) 266-1373
Call for fee information.

Wyoming
Vital Records Services
Hathaway Building
Cheyenne, WY 82002
(307) 777-7591
Birth Certificate: $12.00

APPENDIX B

ANSWERS TO PRE-EMPLOYMENT ASSESSMENT: WHAT DO YOU KNOW?

Answers should have the gist of the following answers. They may be worded differently.

1. What two forms of identification do you need to work legally in the United States?

    You need a document to prove citizenship, such as a certified birth certificate, a Social Security card, and a document to prove identity, such as a state- or federally issued photo ID.

2. What is an employment portfolio and what is its purpose?

    A portfolio is a set of materials designed to show you at your best to an employer. Your portfolio should include a resume, samples or photos of your work, military discharge papers, diplomas or GED certificate, copies of any other certificates or honors you have earned, letters of reference from former employers or contact information for persons who will provide a positive reference, and if not a citizen, alien registration card.

3. What are three ways to find job leads?

    Look in the classified section of the newspaper while you are incarcerated to find out what kinds of companies might be hiring. Ask your parole officer, friends, and members of any support group such as AA or NA. Search the Internet after you have been released, especially Craigslist.

4. What is the Federal Bonding Program?

    The Federal Bonding Program is a government insurance program designed to protect employers if someone who works for them steals money or property. It takes some of the risk out of hiring an ex-offender.

5. How do you get a certified copy of your birth certificate?

   To get a certified copy of your birth certificate, you need to write to the office of vital statistics in the state where you were born, and provide the name of your mother, date of your birth, and place of your birth—city or county. You will need to send a check or money order to obtain the certified copy.

6. What are three expectations employers may have?

   Among the things employers expect are the following: you will show up on time ready to work, have good attendance, follow instructions, turn off your cell phone, be honest, be helpful to others, and have a positive attitude—no whining.

7. What is a Targeted Tax Credit for employers?

   The Targeted Tax Credit, a federal program, may make an employer think about hiring ex-offenders in a more positive way. If employers take part in the program, they receive a tax credit of up to $2,400 per worker.

8. What four things can you do prior to your release to prepare for a job?

   To prepare for a job before reentering the community, you can get a certified copy of your birth certificate, a state ID card, a social security card, and your military discharge papers. Then, you can prepare a mistake-free job application to send to employers, look through the telephone book and newspaper to find where you might want to work, research your chosen field, and ask family members or a counselor to put information you provide on the computer for employers to see.

9. What is an apprenticeship program?

   An apprenticeship lets you learn by doing. You study a career with someone who is already experienced in the field you want to learn. Often, some additional school or training is provided.

10. With a criminal record, are you prohibited from working for yourself?

    No, but see if you need a special license or permit to do so.

11. What is the Oxford House?

The Oxford House is a group living situation run by and for people in recovery. You must apply to live in an Oxford House and show that you are sincere about your substance-abuse recovery, that you can pay your share of the expenses, and that you will attend 12-Step meetings regularly.

12. What is the quickest way to find a job?

The quickest way to find a job is to do all the following: Send out your resume before you are released and follow up on it if you do not hear. Go to the Workforce Employment Centers; look at community bulletin boards and local newspaper classified ads; talk to friends, family, people at your AA/NA meetings (and you may wish to attend a variety of these meetings). Also, think about what needs are not being met in your community and plan how you might help people get what they need or would like.

13. True or false: large companies, such as Target or Home Depot, are the best places to apply for jobs.

False. "Mom and Pop Shops" may look at applicants differently and give you a chance even when you have a record.

14. Name three organizations that could assist you in your reintegration.

There are many organizations such as Salvation Army, Volunteers of America, Catholic Charities, the United Way, Workforce Employment Center or another one-stop career center.

15. What is the minimum recommended time to stay on the job before moving on to another one?

You should stay on a job for at least six-months before moving on to another one. If you feel that you can't take your job another day, you should still give your employer two weeks' notice and not just walk off never to return.

16. How are you going to answer the question, "Have you ever been convicted of a felony?"

This is a tough question, but you should answer it honestly and in your own words. You can practice answering the question while you are still incarcerated. Maybe you will say something such as, "I made a bad choice a few years ago and I was convicted of assault. I've used my time in Wabash Prison to complete my associate's degree as a landscape architect, and that's why I would really like to work at Green Lawn Designs."

17. What types of jobs are more apt to hire felons?

    They include jobs in warehouses, manufacturing, construction, hotels, janitorial services, landscaping, temp-to-hire positions, phone sales, food service, and customer service.

18. What are three ways to improve your knowledge and skills?

    You can improve your knowledge and skills by taking courses, or receiving training completing your GED, and doing some self-directed learning at the library.

19. What is a one-stop career center?

    A one-stop career center is a free government service center where you can find computers to search for jobs, gain information on apprenticeships and other training, and get job search guidance. You can find one by calling (877) USA-2JOBS or visiting www.servicelocator.org.

20. What is a search engine?

    A search engine is a tool on the Internet that helps you find things you are looking for. You use a search engine by typing in key terms, such as "ex-offender jobs."

About the Author

The author, Mike Davis, was in Thailand, where he explored third-world incarceration practices and spiritual fulfillment.

Author and entrepreneur, Mike Davis, tends to appreciate the tough side of life; yet, he does what he can to improve the lives of others. In the early 1990s, he entered the world of the career criminal as a reentry counselor in a halfway house where he was able to help offenders through the transition process from life in prison to life in mainstream society.

In 1997, Mike established the nonprofit, self-supporting 9 to 5 Beats Ten to Life model, "We Believe in Making Our Own Breaks and Making Our Own Money," organization. During the summer of that year, he began selling hot dogs for a buck, using that money to fund a duplex for the express purpose of housing ex-offenders. Over the next twelve years, that small operation has grown from a single duplex to several single-family homes.

After discovering his passion for working with the downtrodden, lost people of society, Mike pursued a master's degree in counseling and began working as a probation and parole officer. Feeling the need to reach more people and educate them, Mike authored the book: *99 Ways to Stay Unemployed* and the following videos/DVDs: *Tough Questions & Straight Answers, Out for Good,* and the first version of this book, which are available from ACA. When he is not buried up to his elbows in the usual paperwork, Mike travels to third-world countries that are not as lucky as ours, learning about their criminal justice system, and he reminds himself of what real humanity, perseverance, and strength exists in the world.

Mike would like to hear from you. Please send your suggestions and success stories based on this book to fromcontocareer@yahoo.com or mail them to:

Mike S. Davis
PO Box 56571
Virginia Beach, VA 23456